The **SHAMAN'S MIND**

The
SHAMAN'S
MIND

HUNA WISDOM TO CHANGE YOUR LIFE

Jonathan Hammond

Monkfish Book Publishing Company
Rhinebeck, New York

The Shaman's Mind: Huna Wisdom to Change Your Life © 2020
by Jonathan Hammond

Paperback ISBN 978-1-948626-21-7
eBook ISBN 978-1-948626-22-4

Library of Cataloging-in-Publication Data

Names: Hammond, Jonathan, Shamanic practitioner, author.
Title: The shaman's mind : Huna wisdom to change your life / Jonathan
  Hammond.
Description: Rhinebeck, New York : Monkfish Book Publishing Company, 2020.
  | Includes bibliographical references.
Identifiers: LCCN 2020000478 | ISBN 9781948626217 (paperback) | ISBN
  9781948626224 (ebook)
Subjects: LCSH: Huna. | Shamanism--Hawaii.
Classification: LCC BF1623.H85 H36 2020 | DDC 299/.9242--dc23
LC record available at https://lccn.loc.gov/2020000478

Book and cover design by Colin Rolfe
Cover painting: "Plantas Medicinales" by Anderson Debernardi
Ho'oponopono Diagram by James Donegan | Jamesdidit.net

Quote on page 152 from *The Drama of the Gifted Child: The Search for the True Self*
by Alice Miller copyright © 2008, 1994. Reprinted by permission of Basic Books,
an imprint of Hachette Book Group, Inc.

A portion of the proceeds for this book will be donated to
Hawaii Wildlife Fund
P.O. Box 790637
Paia, HI 96779
WildHawaii.org

Monkfish Book Publishing Company
22 East Market Street, Suite 304
Rhinebeck, NY 12572
(845) 876-4861
monkfishpublishing.com

This book is dedicated to Serge Kahili King, Brian McCormack, and my mother.

CONTENTS

PART THREE
The **THREE SELVES**

PART FOUR
HO'OPONOPONO

PREFACE

This book is about becoming a finder and no longer a seeker.

It's about truly healing. It's about learning to love yourself; to think straight; to step into wellness, prosperity, and love; and to feel the inner satisfaction of these attainments to such a degree that the inevitable response is to give yourself back to the world. Imagine yourself so well, so full, and so supported, that you can't help but want to spread your good fortune around.

In every given moment, each of us has a glorious opportunity to release our self-limiting stories, learn to live from our true nature, and become the highest and brightest expression of ourselves. And I know of no better, more practical, or more effective system to guide you there than Huna, the esoteric knowledge and philosophy of Hawaii.

We are currently in the midst of an immense, difficult, and sometimes terrifying planetary shift of consciousness. We are on the brink of complete unsustainability—we cannot continue our current ways without careening toward destruction. The Cree tribe of North America speaks of a contagious psychospiritual disease of the human soul—a virus or parasite of the mind that is currently manifesting itself in the form of unprecedented conflicts and crisis on a global scale. This wicked spirit, which terrorizes and cannibalizes others, is called Wetiko or the Wetiko Virus. In Hawaiian, it is referred to as 'E'epa, which means "deceit that passes comprehension."

Wetiko/'E'epa is born of our disconnection from the natural world and it operates by covert infestation of the human psyche, compelling us, through toxic selfishness, to act against our own best interests by blinding us to our own insanity: destruction for profit, massive hoarding of wealth, allowing suffering without compassion, dehumanizing others, and recklessly exploiting natural resources.

Wetiko, however, is non-local. In other words, it doesn't have any substantive, material existence except in our own minds. This points to an incredible intrinsic power and deep personal responsibility within each of us to make a difference in this world by cultivating our own individual consciousness, by cleaning up our own mess and making ourselves so well so that we can have a positive influence on all of life, and on all of those whom we touch.

Quantum physics posits the Quantum Inseparability Principle— every atom effects every other atom, everywhere, because everything influences everything else in every direction and every which way in time. This means that everything we do matters; how we think and live has energetic reverberations that affect all beings everywhere. The microcosm of our individual selves *is* the macrocosm of the entire planet and beyond. There is no separation.

I can only guess that if you are holding this book, you feel a deep calling and personal need to be part of the global solution. And because we are all inseparably connected in this one universe, even the simple yearning to live our best lives contributes vitally toward this deeper intentionality. In the last fifty years we have become inundated with consciousness-expanding, esoteric wisdom from a host of indigenous and spiritual traditions, and for good reason. A contemporary spiritual movement, an army of "light workers" is being formed to prepare and fortify millions for the changes ahead.

This has already been prophesied.

The Quechua people, who live in the Andes of South America, call the time in which we are now living the Fifth Pachacuti. A Pachacuti is a five-hundred-year interval, and this particular one is an era in which, as the legend states, the Eagle and the Condor will fly together in the same sky. According to the Quechua, the previous two thousand years were dominated by the Eagle—a visionary, but materialistic bird; one connected to seeing vast distances, the intellect, and the masculine principles of growth and movement. Over the last two thousand years, the Eagle's influence was seen in the huge advancements and discoveries that took place in science, medicine, and technology.

But the Fifth Pachacuti, which we now inhabit, is a time when the feminine, spiritual, and environmentally-minded Condor will begin to dance together with the Eagle, restoring balance and harmony with her intuitive Earth wisdom. The Quechua believe that the Condor embodies such sacredness that she might not actually fly, but can somehow spiritually move herself.

In the Quechan prophecy, during the Fifth Pachacuti, the entrance of the Condor will come about with the help and support of those humans who espouse Earth-honoring ways, those who live in right relation with themselves and their environment, and those who choose to lean into the interconnectivity of all things.

And that is you.

The best way to fight the Wetiko/'E'epa demon is to start by naming it. By naming it, we diminish its power. Then we can lend ourselves, through the inner rainbow light of our hearts and minds, to anyone—and anything—which, for whatever reason has lost their way or had their freedoms diminished.

We do this not only through the actions we take in the world, but by cultivating a consciousness within our own minds that always leads us toward choice, possibility, and the highest levels of inclusivity. The Hawaiians call this consciousness *Aloha*. The word *Aloha* is a commonplace greeting in Hawaii, and it is often translated as "love," but it has great spiritual significance as well. In Hawaii, Aloha is considered an attitude, an ethic, and a means for change. It means to share life force with another, using the essence of love as an expression of our life force in order to further creation.

This is an utterly natural process, because creation itself, as you will find in the pages that follow, is made of the very stuff that is Aloha, the love that is in alignment with what we consider to be the most elevated qualities of Spirit: grace, forgiveness, compassion, gentleness and kindness.

To learn to infuse your thinking mind, and therefore your external life, with the potent force of Aloha is to do your part to confront Wetiko/'E'epa and help the Condor lift off to the tallest and most transcendent heights. If enough of us learn to do this for ourselves, the Wetiko/'E'epa demon will be no match for what we can accomplish individually and globally.

It's time for real and substantive change, which only you can make for yourself. It's been said that there is nothing new under the sun, and I am convinced that the ocean of spiritual books, classes, workshops, and internet programs that are now so readily available mean absolutely nothing if we don't dig in and do our own personal work with gusto. It's time to let go of what I call "weekend spiritual adventures," or reading the latest self-help gurus so that we can sound interesting at cocktail parties. The invitation rather, is to learn to change your mind. By doing so, you will awaken an inner shamanic self that moves in alignment with the most beneficent and powerful forces of Nature and Spirit. This is the essence of Huna, and the overall aim of contemporary shamanic practice.

But if you don't feel a particular connection to the Hawaiian Islands, pay that no mind. I often refer to Hawaiian Shamanism as

"Shamanism with better beaches." The wisdom contained in this book transcends the culture from which it came because it points to universal truths that open us to love, and as we open, so does the world. Even though we will address both in great depth, this is not just a book on Huna or Hawaii. My aim is to use both as a framework to introduce much broader psychological, spiritual, and healing perspectives.

If you are reading this, you are operating under some vestige of freedom—at the very least, you have enough choice and space in your life to delve into this material, and choose what you want to do with it. But there are so many beings—people, rivers, animals, oceans, and trees—who for whatever reason don't have that same luxury.

So read this book for them. Show up for yourself for them. Make yourself well for them. Awaken your interior magic for them. It's definitely you first, but they all need you too. Because the truth is, we as a collective no longer have time for you not to do this.

Me ke aloha,
Jonathan

PART ONE

INTRODUCTION to **HUNA**

CHAPTER ONE

MY HAWAII STORY

Given that I am a *Haole*—a non-Polynesian white person—living in New York City, without a drop of Hawaiian blood in my body, it seems relevant to offer some clarification as to how I have found my way to Huna. My connection to Hawaii is actually something that I am still trying to understand—a perplexing web of crazy synchronicities, gut instinct, and happy accidents. And yet, as true as it is that I found Hawaii, I can't deny that Hawaii somehow also found me.

Sharing my story is not an act of self-indulgence; it is a teaching in and of itself, one that is loaded with the hidden and mysterious realities that we often deny or refuse to see. Realities that, if we choose to be open to them, point toward the deeper tendrils of connectivity and intelligence that underlie all things. "Limitlessness," or infinite connection, is one of the seven major principles of Huna, so as I introduce my Hawaii story to you, I will likewise introduce you to the seven principles.

To delve into Shamanism is to open to an inner knowing that lies beyond what we are able to learn from books, teachers, or the culture to which we believe we should adhere. "All power comes from within" is another major Huna principle, and following this inward direction became my path to this knowledge.

By the time I reached my late thirties, I had been on the spiritual and healing path for almost two decades—and I needed to be. I had been through periods of severe anxiety and depression, the difficult end of a thirteen-year relationship, and struggles with addiction. I did not have an easy go of things. The more I healed, the more I found myself unfortunately settled in a career that felt out of alignment with who I was becoming spiritually. I was restless, searching, and sometimes quite angry. Up to that time, I had spent the majority of my life as a professional actor, appearing on Broadway and on stages across the country, and I had done a little television as well. I loved being an artist, but I struggled with a lifestyle that was financially difficult, lacked opportunity, and felt disempowering.

Despite relative success, acting was generally a difficult slog. I often felt judged, rejected, and compromised. Even worse, it was becoming clear that I needed to compartmentalize and hide my spiritual life and my work as an energy healer. My theatrical agent told me that the "woo-woo stuff" made me a lot less marketable. There was a faint whisper within me that questioned whether I should stop acting. After all, since early childhood, it had been the only thing I ever thought I wanted. Giving it up felt like an identity crisis, so every time the idea of quitting came into my head, I would banish it immediately.

That is, until I went to Maui.

Haleakala Volcano

I had been to Hawaii a few times before the events that I am about to describe and had absolutely loved it. I can lose myself fairly easily being in Nature, and the sumptuous paradise of the islands provided unparalleled delights. I loved the emerald green hills and rainbow valleys, the crystal blue and indigo water, the delectable smells of wild flower perfumes, the misty sea salt sprays, the cleansing rains, the cloud-capped mountains, and the busy click-click-click of palm trees singing their songs through invisible tropical winds. If you haven't been to Hawaii, I highly recommend it.

But other than my delight in Hawaii's natural wonders, I had acquired no knowledge whatsoever of Hawaiian spirituality, language, or culture. The Hawaiian words on street signs or restaurants seemed cumbersome and almost too foreign. Like most tourists, I had a vaguely titillating awareness of the lithe, pretty girls and the tattooed, muscular men wiggling their hips in exotic Hula movements, but I was quite unaware of Hula's deeper meanings, and I certainly never dreamed that the islands contained a spiritual philosophy that would become such an important part of my life.

Despite my lack of knowledge of many aspects of Hawaii, there was an internal experience that I had on those early trips to these islands, and have had every time since. I call it my "Hawaii feeling." In my deepest being, it tells me, "These islands are the most magical place on Earth, and I am only complete if I somehow carry them with me always." Many Hawaiian words contain hidden meanings or concealed references that are buried within them; these are called *kaona*. If you examine the kaona, of the word Hawai'i it is understandable why I and so many others are so drawn to return there again and again. *Ha* is the word meaning the breath of life to man, *Wai* means the water of life to the earth, and *'I* is the Supreme Being. Hawai'i, or Hawaii, as we more commonly spell it, is the homeland which all mankind continues to seek because it is there that life, Earth, and Spirit conjoin together.

My story begins on the volcano in Maui. Getting to the Haleakala Crater, Maui's dormant volcano, which had its last eruption in 1790, involves a dizzying thirty-five-mile drive into the clouds, up ten thousand feet on a road that twists and turns so abruptly that speed limits often max out at ten miles per hour. Many tourists do this drive in the middle of the night in order to be at the summit for sunrise, which I find rather terrifying because one's vehicle is sometimes only a few yards away from a thousand-foot drop.

On my first trip to Haleakala, with my husband Domenic, we reached the top after almost two hours. When we got out of the car we could not believe where we were and what we were seeing. Among the many lessons one receives from the land of Hawaii is just how small we are. At the Haleakala Crater, the hole, so to speak, where the lava once gushed forth, is the size of Manhattan. To stand at the edge is to view a gigantic, sparkling kaleidoscopic landscape of rolling rock and soil that appears to undulate in wave-like patterns of other-worldly greens, reds, purples, and browns for as far as the eye can see. It is breathtaking.

Being there makes you feel like you're on another planet, or perhaps the moon, and the bright, shiny Haleakala Silversword plants, which only grow on the crater and nowhere else on Earth, add to the otherworldly nature of this magnificent place. You never know what to expect in terms of weather at the summit, and having been there many times now, I can attest to rain, snow, clouds so thick that you can't see anything, freezing temperatures, and hot sun. But on the day I visited for the first time, it was warm and clear with high visibility.

In addition to the astonishing scenery, there is an energy at the summit that I have never experienced anywhere else. The land itself has a visible and pulsating aura or luminous field, almost like the heat waves that come of an asphalt highway in the desert, but mystically different. Pele, the volcano goddess of Hawaii, now lives on Big Island, where there are four active volcanoes. Although she is often thought of as ferocious and wrathful, her presence on Maui has a sense of sweet and tranquil luminescence, as if her work on this island is done and she is now at peace here.

In addition to the astonishing scenery, there was a strange sound in the air, an extremely high-pitched ringing—"zzzzzzzzzz"—that felt like it was the sound of silence itself. It had an oddly faint and deafening quality at the same time, as if it were somehow sonically cleaning my ears and sinuses. I couldn't believe that none of the other visitors there seemed to notice this sound, but once I pointed it out to Domenic, he heard it too.

Before we began walking the long and well-worn path down into the crater, we found a posted sign explaining that the ancient Hawaiians considered Haleakala (which means "House of the Sun" in Hawaiian) an extremely sacred place. The sign spoke of a time when only the Kahunas, or Hawaiian shamans, were allowed to come there, because the crater held so much *Mana*, or power. The sign also stated, rather mysteriously, that when the holy men and women of old would come to Haleakala, they would do so only for what they needed, and when they received it—a message, an omen, an answer—they would leave immediately. The other tourists walked past this sign, paying it no notice—and oddly, the last time I was there the sign was gone—but I felt like it was giving me the very instructions that I needed to experience this place in the proper way.

We hiked Haleakala in silence (except for the "*zzzzzzz*") for quite a while, stopping along the way to pause, breathe, and behold the majesty around us. I definitely lost all sense of time, and when I pulled my cell phone out of my pocket to check, it read 12:34. The first of the seven principles of Huna states, "The world is what you think it is." These kinds of numerological synchronicities mean something to me—I choose to think they do, so they do. Seeing 12:34 set off an inner signal that told me it was time to stop and sit down.

Looking up, I found myself at the edge of a picturesque plateau with knee- and waist-high lava rock all around me. This seemed like the spot. I lost sense of where Domenic was, but my instinct was that he was probably having his own experience. Sitting on sharp lava rock can be dicey. It is born of fire, and its roughness is a physical manifestation of the "burn" that is still inside it. Because it can cut easily, I placed a towel underneath me, got into as comfortable a seated position as I could, and entered into a light meditation.

I don't know exactly how long I was sitting there, but suddenly, from out of nowhere, a roaring force began rushing toward me as if a speeding train was headed straight in my direction, and I was on the tracks in its path. This wasn't an internal feeling or inner vision; this was a visitation with something so powerful that I found that I could no longer sit up. An invisible push forced me to lie back, and as I did, the unforgiving lava rock seemed to cradle my body as if I were on the most comfortable reclining chair in the world. I was instantaneously in a visual white-out and could not see my hand in front of my face. I knew that I was being surrounded by clouds, but something else inexplicable was happening around and inside me.

My consciousness became ephemeral and spacious. I began to feel light-headed, nauseous, and not a little frightened. I was coming face to face with what I can only call IT. God, Source, Great Spirit, the Mother—whatever you want to call it—IT was there, and I could do nothing but allow IT to wash through the very fabric of my being. I experienced wildly unfamiliar physical sensations and feelings as a dreamlike experience of altered awareness overtook my mind and body.

A spontaneous life review, the kind that people are said to experience at the moment of their death, ensued. Thre wasn't anything I could hold on to, make sense of, or control. I was experiencing Relative Reality, the implied opposites contained in all things simultaneously: tears and laughter, past and future, regret and hope, terror and peace, all at once.

And then something even stranger happened: I had the realization that IT knew what was happening. Not only was I aware of IT, but IT was aware of me. And I knew that IT knew that I knew this!

I remained with IT for as long as IT chose to stay with me (I think it was only about thirty minutes, although I can't know for sure), and when IT left, I remained unmoving in the same position for some time.

I knew that something had shifted deeply, but I hadn't even begun to process it. I wanted to remember the exact place that I was in, so without getting up, I began to take pictures with my cellphone all around my head and shoulders so that I had some record of where I had met IT. What I was to find out when I got back to my hotel was that in those pictures, right next to my head, was the unmistakable face and shell of a turtle, my totem animal, carved into the lava rock by the elements, smiling at me. When I saw it, every hair on my body stood on end.

After the IT experience was over, I found Domenic, who had also had his own profound encounter, although very different than mine, with IT. I remembered the instructions from the sign, and I knew that I had certainly received what I had come for. Now it was time to go, and we began walking back along the path, both of us awestruck by what had just occurred.

As we hiked, with our consciousness still feeling slightly altered, we both saw flying red and purple things in our peripheral vision, but when we would turn our heads quickly to follow them, there would be nothing there. Haleakala was sharing some of its secrets with us on that day, and bizarre and strange phenomenon—faces in cloud formations, strange sounds, and tricks of vision—continued on our return journey up the volcano's crater slope.

We walked in silence for a while and then I suddenly blurted out, "I want to be a full-time healer and teacher. I want to quit acting, and I want to run spiritual retreats around the world." At the very moment that these words exited my lips, a tiny dust tornado formed on the path right in front of us. It lifted up into the air, hovering a few feet from the ground, and then whizzed away in a flash with a "zing!" Domenic and I looked at each other, wide-eyed and slack-jawed. "Well, alrighty then!" I exclaimed.

In the years that followed, I did exactly what I said I would do on that volcano. The third principle of Huna says, "Energy flows where attention goes," and I put all my attention and focus into changing my life. I went full-steam ahead with some formal education that I still needed, and dove even more deeply into shamanic practice.

In no time I opened a spiritual counseling and healing practice in New York City that now operates with a wait-list. I started a travel company, leading spiritual retreats around the world. The preeminent teacher and author Llyn Roberts asked me to join her core faculty for Shamanic Reiki Worldwide, and I began teaching Shamanism and Reiki in major venues across the country. I never looked back on acting. Once I had made the choice, it just faded into the distance. The fifth Huna principle says, "Now is the moment of power." I caught up with myself by fully acknowledging who I had now become, and this allowed me to release a past self that existed only in memory.

During those early years as a shamanic teacher and practitioner, I still hadn't found Huna. Shamanism, to my mind, lived in Central and

South America. I previously had held an apprenticeship with some of the shamans of Brazil to work with their plant medicine, and the retreats I was leading were mainly to Latin countries. Despite my love affair with Hawaii, I never thought to look there for spiritual influence. But later I would find out that I was practicing Huna without knowing that I was doing so. The next step to this realization happened on a shamanic journey that would eventually take me to the island of Kauai.

Kauai and the Aumakua

Shamanic journeys are the cornerstone of my shamanic practice; they are how I most easily connect with spirit guides and healing wisdom. (How to journey will be covered later in this book.) One day, on a break between clients, I decided to do a journey in my office. I lay down, lowered the lights, covered my eyes, and allowed myself to be taken wherever my psyche and spirit wanted me to go. After a few minutes, I found myself in what seemed to be Hawaii, but the landscape was quite different than anything I had seen before. I certainly had never been in this particular place in real life.

This landscape was the same Hawaiian green that I knew so well, but its hills and slopes were larger and more dramatic. There were magnificent and insurmountable sea cliffs that were unfamiliar to me, but I now realize that I was seeing the Napali coast of Kauai. My journey took me to a lush and verdant meadow, where a stunningly beautiful Polynesian woman, complete with a Plumeria flower behind her ear, was performing an elegant dance to the gods of the place. As she saw me approach, she said smilingly, "Come to Kauai, you have ancestors here." A moment later, she faded away, and I came out of the journey with a start.

Now, I was fairly certain that I did not have ancestors in Hawaii; I'm Italian-Irish and from Michigan. But the first principle of Huna says, "The world is what you think it is," and I believe that shamanic journeys connect us to deep wisdom and truth, so I felt that my only choice was to set out to discover what this woman meant. Domenic and I had another trip to Maui planned in around six weeks' time, so I immediately called him. "Dom, we need to go to Kauai, not Maui," I told him. "I had a shamanic journey and a Hawaiian woman told me that's what I should do because I have ancestors there." Domenic is used to me, and puts up with my antics most generously. So, even though he probably rolled his eyes on the other end of the phone, he agreed and changed our reservations.

From a shamanic perspective, the word "ancestors" can mean many things. While it typically points toward bloodlines, ancestors can also be lineages that we relate to spiritually—our spirit family, so to speak, rather than our real one. We can often recognize ancestral currents simply by observing which traditions of wisdom attract us, and they can even reveal themselves through aesthetics that we admire—Buddhist art, Peruvian fabrics, or Sufi music can all point us toward the ancestral lines within us.

Our high self (*Kane* in Hawaiian) holds all that we ever were, and all that we will ever be. It is a guiding and connecting higher personal spirit that acts as a mediator between each of us and the cosmos. Kane contains the soul material that makes up the totality of our limitless being. It is the part of us that never dies, and as the Hawaiian phrase *hanau wawa*, which means reincarnation, suggests, Kane creates our many lives in such a way as to maximize the lessons our soul is to learn in whatever lifetime we happen to be experiencing.

In Hawaiian cosmology, Kane relates directly to the *aumakua*, the ancestors—and not just *our* ancestors, but *all* ancestors. "*Po'e aumakua*" in Hawaiian means "the great company of ancestors," or the higher selves of all beings. Carl Jung had a similar idea in his concept of a shared and hereditary memory and consciousness between all humans that he termed the "collective unconscious." The second

Huna principle states, "There are no limits," which means that there is a connection to everything if you can somehow find it.

So I went to Kauai to find my ancestors.

But by the sixth morning of our seven-day trip, I was feeling disappointed. Despite spending a glorious time on the lush garden isle of Kauai, there were definitely no ancestors to be found. Nada. I had all but given up on what was seeming like a rather silly quest, but since "Energy flows where attention goes," the third principle of Huna, I kept my eyes open, despite feeling that the search for my ancestors seemed futile.

We had already seen most of the main sites on Kauai, but the second-to-last day of our trip was reserved for a visit to Waimea Canyon, which Mark Twain once called, "the Grand Canyon of the Pacific." Seventy-five percent of Kauai is inaccessible on foot and uninhabitable. Waimea Canyon is on the east side of the island. From where we were staying, in Princeville on the north end, we couldn't drive to it directly, but had to circumnavigate the entire island. It turned out to be worth the effort, because the drive up the canyon revealed amazing scarlet rock waterfalls and spectacular views.

Waimea Canyon itself is remarkable. On its precipice is a cliff-side that plunges straight down almost four thousand feet. Standing close to the edge of it is like being on the tallest floor of a New York skyscraper with no windows and nothing to break your fall. It felt dangerous to stand too close to the edge, and it made me queasy; I only felt comfortable by staying a few feet back.

On the day that we visited the canyon, we were alone, without another soul in sight. I found a large rock to sit on, and quietly communed with the spectacular views of immense purple, green, and red walls of earthen forest, cliffs, and valleys.

As I sat there, a man appeared, seemingly from out of nowhere, and approached us. He looked like a typical tourist, possibly from the Midwest, wearing a bright Tommy Bahama Hawaiian shirt and a silly white fedora hat. He was rather jolly, and, with a big smile, came up to me and asked if I would take his picture. I was kind of "having a moment," connecting with the canyon, and he was definitely interrupting my meditative state, but I hid my haughty annoyance and politely agreed.

As he stood there, posing for the picture with his back to the canyon, just a foot or two from the cliff's steep drop-off, he suddenly took a startled breath, and intuitively grabbed his chest when he realized how close he was to the edge. He moved further away from the precipice and a little closer to me, and gave me a wide-eyed look, saying, "Wow, that cliff is intense."

"I know! It is scary, right? It's straight down for thousands of feet!" I said.

His smile faded, and his face became rather serious. Locking his blue eyes on mine and taking an audible breath as if to center himself, he said, "If your ancestors hadn't taught you to be afraid of this cliff, you wouldn't be here to take my picture."

I felt slightly faint, and probably turned white. I looked straight at him, and asked him to repeat what he had just said. As if he were waiting for this request, he calmly said again, "If your ancestors hadn't taught you to be afraid of this cliff, you wouldn't be here to take my picture."

Speechless and dumbfounded, I took his picture and handed him back his camera, somehow finding a way to conceal the shock that I felt. His only other words were, "Have a good day!" and then he vanished as quickly as he had appeared. Domenic, who had observed the whole interchange said, "Was he even real?" to which I replied, shaking my head, "I have absolutely no idea."

Later that day, while sunbathing at Hanalei Bay, I suddenly jumped up and ran to the ocean. I had felt Turtle's presence and went to investigate. Within a few minutes, I found all one hundred and fifty pounds of her, eating sea grasses in less than three feet of water. We stayed together for quite a while, and she didn't swim away, but was warm and friendly to my presence. It was a heart-centered exchange for both of us, and it epitomized the fifth Huna principle, *Aloha*, which states, "To love is to be happy with"—in other words, to love is to share love with another.

I didn't know then that many Hawaiian families believe that, in addition to loved ones who have passed on, certain animals and even elementals—stone, fire, etc.—are part of their aumakua, or totemic spirit family. Given that this was a special day of feeling into an ancestral stream that was all new to me, it was an incredible gift to make contact with an animal ally that was such an important part of my shamanic path.

By the way, I know that there are some schools and teachers of Shamanism that hold it to be improper to reveal one's animal totem to others. That isn't a belief that I hold, so it isn't true for me. I instinctively know that Turtle wouldn't mind either. "The world is what you think it is." What's true is only what is true for you.

My aumakua experiences with the odd man on Waimea Canyon and with Turtle in Hanalei Bay had a lasting impact that validated something within myself that didn't yet make sense, yet was impossible to deny. My connection to Hawaii began to transcend my natural affinity for the islands, for the land was starting to live inside my bones. I began to seek out books and resources on Hawaii's indigenous spirituality, and the more I learned, the more I found direct corollaries to my own shamanic understanding and ways of working. Huna felt like a homecoming, an inexplicable affinity for material that I should not have known, but somehow already did.

Discovering Huna and Ho'oponopono

When I began studying Huna, I was already feeling quite pleased with myself about what I was accomplishing in my private practice. I considered myself a skilled, knowledgeable, and effective healer, and I was seeing substantive results with clients, making good money, and feeling "cutting edge" in what I thought was my own unique blend of psychology, somatics, the chakras, Shamanism, and energy healing. However, my inflated ego took quite a blow when I started to realize that everything that I thought I knew, as well as many of the contributions made by Freud, Jung, and a host of other pioneers in the fields of psychology and healing, had long been discovered, at least in part, by the ancient Hawaiians.

Furthermore, unlike many philosophical or spiritual systems that claim to be the only legitimate path, Huna has a flexibility and permissiveness that encourages experience through gnosis. Gnosis is our own personal knowledge or insight into humanity's spiritual mysteries that doesn't come from what we are told, or even believe in. Gnosis is conscious, experiential knowledge, rather than intellectual belief or theory. We each possess a unique inner compass, a deep internal knowing, that is born of the personal experience we have with ourselves and the world. Our gnosis can't be argued with, it just is what it is, and I was so surprised to find this indigenous philosophy from across the ocean that encourages it.

With its seven principles, Huna was providing me with a multi-perspectival system of esoteric wisdom whose philosophical tenets are built upon developing an intimate relationship with one's own creativity, insight, and experience. Huna helped me to clarify and bring language to what it is to think like a shaman and to begin to teach others to do the same. And along with connecting me to a lineage of others who were trafficking in similar currents, it introduced me to *Ho'oponopono*, which was to become among the most powerful healing practices I have ever encountered.

If I were to categorize the overarching methodology of my healing practice, I might call it something like "spiritual re-parenting." When a client presents with a longstanding problem, pattern, or self-limiting story, we seek to find its origin together—where or when did the client first learn that they were unlovable, wrong, not good enough, unworthy? These entrenched patterns almost always trace back to childhood, and to go back to the source of the issue—attending to "the child within"—can be a transformative way of relating to oneself.

There are many Western terms for this kind of therapeutic approach, including "inner child work," "reframing of the past," and "soul retrieval." Ho'oponopono, the Hawaiian forgiveness process (which will be covered in depth later in this book) is a simple and potent practice that achieves these ends with directness and efficiency; it's a kind of "map" that demonstrates the magical alchemy of what love can do. To co-create our lives with support from the benevolent spiritual intelligences that want nothing more than to lovingly assist us back to our wholeness, is to practice Ho'oponopono.

Before I formally trained in Ho'oponopono, my first introduction to it was through a five-minute YouTube video. Huna seems to merge immediately with my intuitive understanding. Based on the information from the video, I created a Ho'oponopono practice that I could use with my clients, and which I still use.

The day that I first decided to experiment with Ho'oponopono with some of my clients, the results were beautiful, and I was quite surprised by just how positive they were. Everyone that I brought through the process experienced a gentle and deeply healing reclamation of themselves. Even more surprising was that as we did Ho'oponopono together, I, as well as some of my clients, sensed a palpable "presence" around us, as if the process was inviting in a kind of spiritual energy or grace that seemed to fill the room. Even the lights in my office would sometimes flicker and shift. To this day, I often experience these kinds of phenomena when I am guiding someone in the Ho'oponopono process, and the first time it happened, it seemed to be synchronistic evidence of the legitimacy and potency of a practice that would eventually become the foundational model for my healing work.

But then I got scared. I had no training in Ho'oponopono, I was clearly trafficking in some intense energy, and I didn't exactly know what I was doing. (I had only watched a YouTube video, for goodness sake!) I went to talk to my supervisor, Brian, who I had been working with for almost twenty years. Brian is a primary spiritual influence in my life. He is among the wisest people I know, and if I ever say anything clever, it probably came from him first. We began our conversation as therapist and client, and now our relationship has taken on a professional affiliation. These days, he is the person I talk to about client work, ethics, and standards of practice. Even though I am not a clinician, I have a large practice, and I find his supervisory support vitally important. Plus, sometimes you just need someone to talk you off the ledge, and my first experience with Ho'oponopono was one of those times.

After I told Brian about what had happened when I used Ho'oponopono with my clients, I said to him, "But Brian, this can't be right, I have no idea what I am doing, I just watched a YouTube video. I'm a fraud!"

"Well, yes, but you said it worked, right?" he replied.

"Like gangbusters," I said, "but I don't know exactly why."

"Relax," he replied. "Keep doing it, and by all means take a class to make yourself feel better. But it's clear that you have tapped into something universal, and you seem to instinctively already know how to do this."

Brian's advice pointed toward the sixth and seventh principles of Huna. The sixth says, "All power comes from within." I already had the knowledge. It couldn't *not* be inside me, because everything was already inside me . As my wonderful shamanic teacher Llyn Roberts often says to her groups, "The wisdom is in the circle," meaning there is no hierarchy between her and her students; she has nothing to teach that isn't already held and known in the group. The seventh Huna principle states, "Effectiveness is the measure of truth." In other words, if it works—as Hoʻoponopono certainly did with my clients—then it's real. In fact, I have heard my magnificent Huna teacher, Serge Kahili King, Ph.D., exclaim, "If it works, then it's Huna!"

Now, I am not claiming that all you have to do is watch a YouTube video and then you can run out and open a healing practice, although I am definitely a bit of a mad scientist when it comes to this stuff. But, often, in my trainings, participants don't take what they learn back into their everyday lives because they are either afraid that they might do it incorrectly or they lack the confidence or self-esteem that gives them permission to try.

As I mentioned in the preface, so much esoteric wisdom that was once considered "secret" is now readily available to the masses. The intelligences of the Universe know what they are doing, and if you have found your way to any of it, you owe it to yourself to try it out at your current level of understanding and development. Don't worry about it, just try it. Remember the fourth Huna principle, "Now is the moment of power." Use the practices you learn in this book in the present moment, and they will work for you too!

The Psychics in My Office

During the time when I was enmeshing myself in all things Hawaiian, I was allowing a talented group of psychics and mediums to rent my office on Friday nights for a bimonthly practice circle. I myself had little to do with the group, and I only attended intermittently—and when I did, I kept to myself and allowed myself to be a student. The participants had a vague notion that I was a healer, but they didn't know me well, and I hadn't shared with anyone that I had been studying Huna.

One Friday night when I didn't attend the circle, I stayed home, reading a book about Hawaiian spirituality. (Yes, I know what you're thinking. That *is* the extent to how exciting most of my Friday nights are these days!) Around ten o'clock that evening, the time when the psychics and mediums would have just finished their meeting, I received a text message from the head facilitator: "Great group tonight. Sorry you missed it. And what's going on with Hawaii?"

I looked at my phone, perplexed. As far as I knew, no one in the group had any knowledge about any connection I had to Hawaii. I texted back, "OK, this is weird. Why are you asking me this?"

His reply was, "Well, we had this totally strange thing happen tonight. Everyone was psychically getting all these Polynesian gods and goddesses in your office that they didn't recognize and have never received before. The entire group were on their phones Googling them, and they seem to have been Hawaiian."

By this time, Hawaii synchronicities had become pretty common-place for me, so rather than being stunned reaction, I just laughed. Pretty freaky, right? Well, yes, but if you remember that the first Huna principle is "The world is what you think it is," you will understand why I believed this to be a message of encouragement for me to stay on this path: the *akua* were clearly working with me. And the third Huna principle, "Energy flows where attention goes," showed me that my continued focus on Huna was creating an energetic current with Hawaii that had found its way into my workspace five thousand miles away from the islands.

The Omega Institute

For the past few years, I have been honored to co-facilitate shamanic Reiki programs at the prestigious Omega Institute in Rhinebeck, New York. Omega is arguably the largest holistic learning facility in the world, hosting hundreds of programs each year for tens of thousands of attendees. Llyn Roberts, who has been a faculty staple there for over twenty years, made an introduction for me to meet with the program director to discuss the possibility of them sponsoring my own shamanic program. It is a very exclusive honor to teach at Omega; only the most celebrated spiritual teachers have offerings there.

To say the least, this meeting was a bit of a "big break." My intention was that if I were accepted, I would teach something relatively tried and safe, a curriculum that had been successful in the past. Because it would be my first solo program, I was expecting no more than that I would facilitate a weekend shamanic program either based on Llyn's work or on an aspect of Shamanism that I knew well.

I was definitely nervous before my meeting with Brett Bevel, Omega's program director. Brett is a celebrated author and famous Reiki teacher, and I still feel like I am with a wizard whenever I am in his presence. He has deep connections to Merlin and he writes about them in some of his books. He's a pretty magical guy.

We met in a private room at Omega, and after just a few minutes of chatting, Brett perused my resume slowly, stopping when he got to the Huna and Ho'oponopono training. He pointed at those few lines, shrugged and said, "I think you should teach this."

Now, I had no intention of bringing up Huna in this meeting. I had only just had my first in-person Huna training in Hawaii, and I was absolutely not ready to teach that material because it was still so new to me. But if I'm anything, I'm a little nutty, and almost before the words were out of Brett's mouth, I blurted out, "Yes!" Some secret part of me knew that I could do it, and though it felt daunting, I had over a year to prepare. It was also significant and characteristically synchronistic that out of all the different things that I could offer at Omega, Brett the Wizard, who barely knew me, brought me back to Hawaii.

If I wasn't already a raving "Hunatic," over the next year, I became a genuine, card-carrying one. My goal was to saturate myself in this material to such an extent that Huna would become integrated knowledge. "Energy flows where attention goes." I spent a year and a half preparing for a weekend workshop that ended up being one of the most successful achievements in my life. After teaching that class at

Omega, I returned home to New York City, inspired to write this book. Much of the material presented here is based on that workshop.

About a month before the workshop, and after hundreds of hours of reading, studying, and practicing, I went back to Maui by myself to just be with the land one more time. The Omega class was at the forefront of my mind, and I was still trepidatious. It felt so important that I do a good job, and I wanted some sort of a sign that I was ready.

As I lay on Little Beach, my favorite beach in Maui, I guided myself into a shamanic journey. Despite the fact that Maui is my favorite island, my shamanic journeys always end up in Kauai. This time, I found myself in a cave, deep into the Napali Cliffs in Kauai. Often, on journeys, I visit a muscular, handsome, and slightly gruff Polynesian man who is one of my spirit guides. His cave is clearly shaman's quarters—there are always a fire, luscious smells, and tables filled with herbs, oils, talismans, and other medicinal things. Sometimes he gives me healings; other times he provides me with simple, pithy messages and insights about whatever is going on in my life.

On this particular journey, I asked him if I was ready to teach at the Omega Institute. He furrowed his brow, frowned, and said in his low, raspy voice, "No."

Then he took me to a ceremonial space in his cave where I had not been before, and left me there for a few minutes. When he reappeared, he was wearing traditional Hawaiian garb that was more elaborate than usual—he wore *ti* leaves around his wrists and a *lei* around his neck, adornments of shells and *kukui* nuts, a headdress of feathers, and a beautifully ornamented *kihei* shawl made of tapa cloth (bark cloth). He approached me as I stood in this space, and began chanting beautiful Hawaiian words that were far beyond my understanding. He placed a lei, similar to his own, around my neck, and then brushed some large leaves all over my body, as if he were doing some sort of cleansing. Finally, he stopped and held my shoulders and looked at me with kind, smiling eyes.

He placed his forehead and nose to mine, and we began sharing breath together, something that Hawaiians call *Honi.* The Hawaiians believe that the breath of the nose is purer than the breath of the mouth, because the breath of the mouth has the ability to criticize. To share breath in this way is to share Aloha. After a few moments, he pulled back a bit from me, smiled, and said in his characteristic grunt, "Okay, now you're ready."

In that moment, I opened my eyes. As the blinding Maui sun came flooding in, directly above my head (I was still lying down), a line of 'Iwa or frigate birds, one after another after another, soared in a straight line directly above me. There were literally hundreds of them.

My heart was so full.

I had needed Hawaii to give me permission to teach some of her secret wisdom to others, and with the birds' appearance, I knew that Hawaii was granting me that permission. In her beautiful book *The Hawaiian Oracle: Animal Spirit Guides from the Land of Light,* Huna author Rima A. Morrell writes, "The appearance of the 'Iwa is a sign that you've made contact with your higher self. Your spirit message has been sent." I watched the 'Iwa birds for a long time; eventually, they flew so high that, despite their large size, they became a maze of swirling, tiny dots.

This leads us to the end of my Hawaii story—at least so far—and to the beginning of yours. I hope that you will enjoy learning Huna wisdom and practice with as much enthusiasm and excitement as I experience when I present them to people. Remember that the real purpose of the teachings that follow is to address your thinking mind. The world is an effect of what goes on between your ears. And, like the magical, multitudinous spectrum of possibilities that is Hawaii, your mind can open in similarly expansive ways. If your mind is filled with Aloha, your life will be too.

The best thing about shamans is that they seem to know just about everything about everything: they sniff out healing wherever they can find it, and in just about any instance, and their capacity for love is seemingly endless. To learn to be like them, is to learn to think like they do. When they like what's happening, they make it better, and when they don't, they change it. And so can you.

Breathe, enjoy, explore. *Mahalo.*

CHAPTER TWO

HAWAIIAN COSMOLOGY

Hawaiian cosmology is a vast landscape of myths, gods and goddesses, language, history, and Nature. Because this is a practical book on how to work with your thinking mind to effect change in your life, I will focus on the underpinnings of a few Hawaiian themes in order to guide you to a universal shamanic paradigm—one that transcends Polynesian culture and points toward alternative ways of relating to your life. For our purposes, throughout this book, it is of little importance that you remember the Hawaiian words themselves. Instead, I encourage you to be open to what they might be teaching you about your own life experience.

Shamanism is an embodied path, not an ascendant one. Unlike many of the Eastern mystical traditions, it wasn't developed to transcend worldly existence, but rather to come into harmony with it. Many indigenous cultures hold that each of us come from the stars. Celebrated Hawaiian elder Hale Kealohalani Makua has said that we made that trip on celestial canoes made of light, accompanied by whales and dolphins. At the very least, if the Big Bang went down the way Western science says it did, it's safe to say that we are all made of some sort of star material.

But we left those heavenly realms to be in bodies. Our souls wanted us to experience all of the delights that this magnificent Earth has to offer. The opportunity for you in your current incarnation is to be here now on this planet, and to do whatever you can to enjoy it to the fullest. The earliest indigenous peoples developed Shamanism for extremely practical purposes—to find food and medicine; to live in collaboration with the Earth and each other; to appreciate Nature, both that which surrounds us and our internal natures; to heal and love well; and to connect with the compassionate spirits that help people do all of this with grace. In his workshops, Serge Kahili King, Ph.D., the author of many books on Huna, often speaks of "getting the healing done so that there's more time to party."

And that's the point.

The point is to get to the beach. The point is your love life, your career, your family, your health, your bank account, and your connection with the Earth. And, when you've got all that in order for yourself, helping others with theirs. So the material in this chapter is not an anthropologic examination of Hawaii, rather, I use Hawaii as a metaphor, a template for developing the expansive shaman's mind that is waiting for you just beneath the surface of your everyday awareness.

Before we begin, I'll share a few thoughts about cultural appropriation. You will see in the pages that follow that I use generalized terms such as "the Hawaiians" or "Hawaiian spirituality," and so on. These expressions have a myriad of associations for people, and I am in no way suggesting that I speak for all Hawaiians or the entirety of their spiritual traditions, history, or culture. To do so would be incredibly presumptuous on my part, well beyond the scope of my knowledge, and antithetical to my efforts. Instead, I present universal shamanic truths that are prismatically demonstrated in the Hawaiian paradigm.

This is really no different than Buddhist meditation, Qi Gong, or yoga, among many other spiritual practices finding their way to the West. Western teachers of these modalities seldom, if ever, claim quite the same "authenticity" as those teachers found in Tibet, China, or India, and the best Western teachers would never even attempt to do so. There are slight and inevitable shifts whenever the indigenous wisdom of one culture is translated for the psyche of another, and part of the Western teacher's job is to make cross-cultural correlations as accessible as possible.

What makes any spiritual truth truly universal is its being substantive enough to be built upon, geographically transported, reinterpreted, and, most importantly, cross-referenced with other spiritual traditions. We all benefit greatly by "feeling into" other cultures through our own lens, for it is in discovering the overarching commonalities that we share that allows us to grow together as a global village.

I will never fully understand what it is to be Hawaiian. My hope with this book is to provide a loving portrait of some of the islands' shamanic traditions, particularly those that are echoed cross-culturally, meanwhile, at the same time, remaining well aware that although there may be some who might take exception to my efforts, I make them in the spirit of celebration, reverence, and respect of a land, its people, and its traditions—which I feel Westerners would be wise to learn from and emulate.

My ultimate goal then, is not the impossible task of offering you a definitive vision of Hawaii, but rather to help you awaken an inner paradise of your own making, one that Hawaii exemplifies just by being Hawaii.

The Kahuna and the Student

Offering Huna teachings freely is to do something that it is not traditionally Hawaiian, and is actually contrary to the ways in which this wisdom was typically passed down from one generation to the next. You may have heard the axiom, "When the student is ready, the teacher will appear." While this is true, to a certain extent, from a Huna perspective we think of everything that we experience as a reflection of our thoughts, so the reverse is possibly more appropriate: As Serge Kahili King once said, "When the teacher is ready, the student will appear." The Hawaiian word for "student" is haumana, which has an interpretive meaning indicating that the pupil's willingness to learn gives Mana, or power, to the teacher.

For in Hawaiian tradition, it is the student, through his or her questioning of the Kahuna, or shaman, that guides his or her own path to the knowledge, and empowers the Kahuna to provide just the right curriculum for each individual. The Kahuna doesn't volunteer information, but responds only to questions. I have heard Serge Kahili King say, "You want to be my apprentice? Okay, be my apprentice." And then he'll stare at you, waiting for you to make the next move.

Traditionally, the wisdom-keepers of Hawaii were notoriously tight lipped about sharing Huna. But this wasn't because of a desire to keep it secret. Rather, it was about preserving their culture and its wisdom by holding it in sacredness, imbuing it with value by carrying it close to their hearts with reverence. As with anything that is precious, it was believed that discernment is needed around where and when it is appropriate to allow Huna to be seen.

There was also the influence of discriminatory legislation against certain spiritual practices, instituted by invaders of all kinds and sometimes by the native Hawaiian rulers as well. It wasn't until 1989 that all of the laws against "sorcery," some of which were punishable by a year in prison and a thousand-dollar fine, were finally overturned. Given that Hawaii has historically been victim to much usurpation by the West—and has suffered its own fair share of native in-fighting—many islanders downplayed or even hid their indigenous spiritual knowledge over the years so that it would appear less valuable or powerful to those who would try to eradicate it.

There are stories of early missionaries and others from the West asking the Kahunas about their legendary magic. They would receive vague and shrugging responses from the Hawaiians, who told the Westerners that the ancient ways no longer existed, and possibly never did—downplaying Hawaiian "magic" to be nothing more than local folklore.

But for the serious student, there were practical benefits to this conservative guarding of the knowledge. The fact is that we can't learn what we don't want to learn, and we can't know what we aren't ready to know. Knowledge given at the wrong time is at best knowledge wasted, and at worst knowledge exploited or misused. You will find that to practice Huna effectively requires you to take one hundred percent responsibility for yourself—and this responsibility is not to be taken lightly.

Huna says that everything that happens to you is an effect of your thoughts. What exists within you is mirrored back to you by the outside world, which means that your fingerprints are on absolutely everything that you experience. The fact is, sometimes we don't want to heal or grow, because that would mean that we would have to do something different. Healing and resistance go hand in hand, they are two sides of the same coin, and to take responsibility for yourself is to acknowledge that resistance, and carry on in spite of it.

Neuroscience has identified a default network in the brain that causes us to constantly replay the past and worry about the future. This is a survival mechanism that ensures a continuity of self that remains fixed and unchanged by keeping us in perpetual relationship to a rigid perspective of who we think we are. This is the reason why, when we attempt to make changes in our lives, to meditate, or even just center ourselves, our minds start to chatter incessantly. We are literally hard wired to resist change, even positive change.

Time and time again, I have seen how a client's resistance to their own healing will energetically reveal itself and try to take over. Clients will manifest parades, accidents, traffic jams, or anything else that can prevent them from making it to my office. The proverbial story of "the car breaking down on the way to the healer" exists for a reason. Being on the healing path often leads toward shifts in identity, which can be scary—habits, friends, careers, relationships, and even family members may have to fall away. The biggest success stories that I have witnessed in my clients involve those who approach their healing with honesty, consistency, and care. The path of development is not a straight line, it's a wave of ups and downs, expansions and contractions, and it is only by continually honoring our sincere yearning to grow and create that we stay on that path.

There is great wisdom, then, in the Kahunas not offering information, but only responding to the queries of the students. This puts the responsibility on the student to enter into a present-time process that requires them to feel into their own internal experience for guidance. The Kahunas were also meticulous about responding only to the exact questions being asked and offering nothing more. As the student gained readiness, subtle shifts in their questions would lead to further revelations of deeper dimensionalities embedded in the knowledge.

We each have an intuitive voice inside that lives deep within our body. The Hawaiians call this *Na'au*, which means "guts," "intestines," and, most pointedly, "the heart of the mind." The Na'au is our gut instinct, the seat of our feelings—or, as it is sometimes called, "the second brain." The ancient Hawaiians believed that the intellect and the emotions were essentially one and the same; because from their perspective, there was great wisdom in synthesizing thought and emotion to be in agreement with each other. You have experienced your Na'au at those times in your life when, grappling with an important choice or decision, you go to a wise friend who tells you to "follow your gut," and when you can feel into what it is telling you, you always make the right choice. That's the Na'au.

The Na'au is connected to Nature itself, and when we learn to discern it, it will never steer us wrong. The more we listen to it, the more we are led toward "flow"—the effortless living that comes from being in our authentic truth. This inner compass lives in us, and being on the shamanic path requires that we nurture an intimate rapport with its deep wisdom. The Kahuna tradition of only answering questions from the student ensures that the student really wants to listen to what the Na'au has to say, and will take responsibility for whatever it tells them.

There is a Huna proverb: A'ole ka 'ike I ka halau ho'okahi, or "All knowledge is not taught in one school." In other words, Huna is one path but it is not *the* path. Acquiring knowledge comes not just from teachers or following established systems, but from the creative engagement that we can each choose to have with our lives. Everything that happens to us (even the bad stuff!) is the material through which we step toward enlightenment.

And what is enlightenment, anyway? If you were to follow any legitimate spiritual path to its penultimate conclusion, you would learn two things: that we are all connected, and that we are all God. Now, I can tell you this myself, but it means very little, or possibly nothing at all until you come to decide what it means to you, if it is true for you, what you want to do about it, and if you want to start asking questions about it. That is your work to do. It is only by engaging deeply with our life that we enter into a co-creative relationship with it, one in which the questions that we ask become the path to the deeper truths within.

The Hawaiian Language

Like the islands themselves, the Hawaiian language is a metaphor for the shaman's mind. The point of my linguistic exploration is obviously not to teach you the language, but rather to offer you a snapshot into how the Hawaiian language supports the indigenous thinking of the shaman's mind.

If we contemplate English or the Western languages with which we are most familiar, we see that their primary purpose is to name things and to label experience. There is a linear, fixed quality to Western languages. Their subject-verb-object structure implies something static and apart. Western languages point at life, but fall short in expressing the beingness of it. It's like vacationers grabbing their cell phones to take a picture of a beautiful place, but forgetting to actually look at the beautiful place! A Zen philosopher once said that when a child learns that a bird is called a "bird," that child's experience of bird is forever changed. The very act of naming distances us from the universe.

The simple sentence, "I hit the ball with the baseball bat," implies a separation between me, the ball, and the bat. This takes us away from the unitive consciousness of the shaman's mind which never forgets an interconnective perspective of oneness. The fact is that the ball, the bat, and I cannot exist without each other and the space between us. Further, that simple sentence tells us absolutely nothing about the flesh-and-blood experience of performing that action.

In our language, words can certainly be put together in highly intelligent, and even wildly creative or poetic ways, but the expression of the experience itself is limited because our language can't vibrate experientially. A finger pointing at the moon is not the moon. The moon is the actual lived experience of the moon. That is why when the wonderful spiritual philosopher Alan Watts was asked the question, "What is reality?" he didn't give a verbal answer, he just rang a bell.

The Hawaiian language functions very differently from Western languages. It doesn't point at reality, *it comes at reality from the inside.* To even begin to understand it, we are required to release our habitual way of seeing the world through eyes of limitation and separation and, instead, bring ourselves into a shifted perception that presupposes unity, feels into vibration and energy, and assumes the presence of concealed and hidden truth.

Hawaiian is a relatively simple language. Although there are comparatively few words, they often contain layers of kaona (hidden meanings), ranging from the mundane to the poetic, the metaphysical, and even to the sexual. For example, Hawaiians don't usually tell the tourists that the word Waikiki, the name of a city on the island of Oahu, also means "flowing water," "springing life force," and "spouting semen." This implies the lived experience of Waikiki involves water, vitality, sensuality, and possibly the literal or metaphoric seeds of creation.

While that is a colorfully illustrative example, here is possibly a more elegant one: The Hawaiian word ha'ena can be translated as "red hot" or "hot sun" but it has another meaning, "intense breath." Ha'ena not only depicts the extreme heat of the sun, but it is also the felt reaction from us through our own breath that the hot sun induces. At the beginning of the day, we breathe out "Haaaaa," as we feel the exhilaration of beholding an awe-inspiring sunrise, feeling the sun's warmth on our face. At sunset, we sigh out an entirely different kind of "Haaaaa" as we breathe out relief, peace, and tranquility while watching the sun disappear down below the horizon.

Nouns and verbs do not exist in Hawaiian in the same way that they do in our language. It's not that the Hawaiian language doesn't name things or depict action, but it does so under the presupposition of a connective experience, where everything exists together. The Hawaiian language implies process. There is a Hawaiian proverb that reads, I ka olelo no ke ola, I ka 'olelo no ka make—"In the word is life, in the word is death." Hawaiian words often contain seeds of their opposite meanings, and nuances in almost every syllable can be doubled for emphasis, or altered with the addition of another vowel to reveal other aspects.

In Hawaiian, there are the same five vowels as in English (a, e, i, o, and u), but only seven consonants—h, k, l, m, n, p, w—and the 'okina, a glottal stop that is written as a single open quote—'—and is pronounced similar to the sound between the syllables of "uh-oh." Hawaiian has a fluid movement and melodiousness to it because every word ends in a vowel. The vowels function roughly like verbs, which means that change or movement is implied in every word. In this way, Hawaiian is vibratory and energetic, a closer approximation to the felt experience of reality—a myriad of changing potentialities and limitless prospects in every moment. To see reality in this way is to see through the lens of the shaman's mind.

If we examine the nature of fear, for instance, we see that it is actually nothing more than an adverse reaction in the present moment to a possible future state of permanent "stuckness"—some negative situation that may continue, unchanging, forever and ever. If you bring to mind your worst fear right now, and follow it to the scariest possible consequence, you will find yourself in a story that is bleak and desolate, with no way out.

The Hawaiian word for sickness or illness is ma'i. If we examine other meanings of this word's syllables, we have ma, which means "a state of," and 'i, which can mean "great" plus an interpretive meaning of "hardness, closeness, or stinginess," which might be thought of as "tension." From a Huna perspective, every illness of the body or mind is born of tension, whether that tension be mental, emotional, or physical. But when we remember that change is inherent in everything, as the Hawaiian language reminds us, then we see that the nature of reality itself is change. So, to fear an unchanging permanent state is to fear something that doesn't exist in reality—and to let it go is to release the tension.

This is the quintessence of Huna: replacing a thought form that induces tension with one that produces relief. And when you do this consistently, the thought form that produces relief grows in strength to such a degree that we begin to exist at an energetic frequency in which that thought form transforms itself into a new reality.

The Hawaiian language has no equivalents for the past or future tenses of verbs; everything is linguistically related to the present moment. Serge Kahili King often gets a giggle in his workshops when he explains that an English language sentence like, "I went to the store yesterday to buy milk," is roughly translated in Hawaiian as, "My having gone to the store yesterday to buy milk *is now over.*" Similarly, "I am going to the beach next week to go snorkeling" becomes, "My going to the beach to go snorkeling next week *hasn't happened yet.*" Experience only exists in the present moment, and nothing else exists outside of it. The present moment is often a foreign land for many of us, and the Hawaiian language brings us back to it by not giving us any other alternatives.

There is a saying among the locals in Hawaii that says, "If you don't like the weather, wait five minutes." This isn't an exaggeration, as the Hawaiian Islands encompass twenty-one of the world's twenty-three climate zones. On one occasion, when I visited the Kilauea Volcano on the Big Island, I experienced rain, snow, sun, mist, and a rainbow *while just walking though the parking lot.* The Hawaiian language has over two hundred words for "wind," and eighty of them are just for the winds of Kauai. There is not a single word that indicates the concept of time, but close to sixty Hawaiian words can be used to describe the subtleties of pleasant or unpleasant smells.

The Hawaiian language cracks open the imagination because it points us toward the endless possibilities exemplified by the islands and by life itself. To think like a shaman is to open to the interdimensional discovery available to us in each instant of our lives. Remember that the shaman improves what is going well, and transforms whatever isn't. You may have to wait five minutes to know what your next move is, but if you keep your eyes open, as the Hawaiian language demonstrates, infinite prospects and hidden surprises can't help but reveal themselves.

Creation — The Po, the Ao, and the Kumulipo

The word "shaman" comes originally from the Tungusic tribes of Siberia, and while it is most often defined as an indigenous healer, another esoteric translation is "one who sees in the dark." It is in the darkness that one develops the shaman's mind, for the darkness holds the mystery. The shaman's domain is in the hidden and invisible realms; those in-between places and worlds that the shaman navigates to receive information, retrieve lost power, and commune with the spirits. I often speak of consensus reality being like the one small slice of an apple pie that you're eating, and shamanic reality, the unseen, being equivalent to the entire rest of the pie. There is so much that doesn't meet the eye.

In Hawaiian cosmology, the visible and the invisible coexist together. Manifest reality, Ao (meaning "light" and "day," in Hawaiian), is born out of a vast expanse of creative potential—a womb of inception from which all of life emerges. The Hawaiians call this Po, which is translated as "night" or "darkness," and also, interestingly, as "the realm of the gods." In Hawaiian thought, darkness contains spiritual intelligence, and it is from darkness that life itself springs forth.

In the Western psyche, darkness has a pejorative connotation. The creation story of Genesis in the Old Testament speaks of God separating the light from the dark and calling the light "good." Darkness became synonymous with evil, separate and distinct from "the light," something to be avoided and transcended, or a place where one is exiled for punishment. But for the Hawaiians, the new day begins not at sunrise, but at sunset. It is in the nighttime dream of the Po that creates the waking life of the Ao. Ao also means "enlightened consciousness," and this is significant because it implies that the daytime of our manifest existence is a kind of paradise, or at least it has the potential to be.

Rather than God, Heaven, and Earth being separate from each other, as Genesis suggests ("In the beginning was God and God created the Heaven and the Earth"), according to Hawaiian Shamanism, we are thrust into a shamanic reality that says "Heaven is right here, and God is too," and we can find them by going into our hidden and darkest aspects and allowing them to emerge from there. In his book Psychology and Alchemy, Carl Jung echoes this when he writes, "One does not become enlightened by imagining figures of light, but by making the darkness conscious."

The creation chant of Hawaii, the Kumulipo, translated as "the pattern of the unseen" or "beginning in deep darkness," tells the story of all of the Earth's inhabitants (plants, animals, and people) being birthed during a vast cosmic night. In her book The Sacred Power of Huna: Spirituality and Shamanism in Hawai'i, Rima A. Morell cites a line from the Kumulipo that adds insight into how creation functions: He po uhe'e I ka wawa, which she translates as, "The darkness slips into light." Darkness and light are not polar opposites of an infinite spectrum, a vast distance apart. Instead, creation is like the experience of an actual dawn—the thin veil between night and day is a liminal space so subtle and gradual as to be almost imperceptible.

The shaman's mind opens to the hidden truths of the unseen because, according to this wisdom, there is virtually no distance between what we can perceive and what we can't. From here, we can't help but come upon the spiritual paradox in everything: what seems big is small, what seems strong is weak, what seems easy is difficult, what seems disappointing is beneficial, and every other iteration of opposites that you can imagine.

When I was about twenty-five years old, I played the leading role in a highly acclaimed stage production in Boston. I had received some notoriety for my performance and even won some prestigious acting awards. Some New York bigwigs came to see a performance, and the cast was told that they intended to move the show to New York. This would have catapulted my career.

Not only did that not happen, but when the show was produced in New York, I couldn't even get an audition. After my artistic triumph in Boston, I could not get hired for anything to save my life, and I did not work for an entire year. I went through a major depression that lasted for months. It was during this time that I began to look into meditation and spirituality, and I began working with a psychotherapist.

Little did I know that the hidden reality of one of the greatest disappointments of my life was to be the seed of the book that you're now reading. Had I gotten what I thought I wanted at that time, I would have been sent even further off my path. I would not have started the spiritual search that led me to my truer self and, almost certainly, I would not be typing these words right now. I can track the "failure" of that time in my life to this very moment, and there is a perfection in all of it.

Time and again, I see this dynamic in many clients in my private practice. When someone comes to me who is experiencing extreme difficulties such as relationships breaking up, major career changes, illnesses, or the questioning of long-held values, I know that hidden gifts of the soul are contained in those hardships. A new dream, even if at first it seems like a nightmare, will bring the light of a new awareness to them. I may not tell them this initially, because they may not be ready to hear it, but I always think it because I have never known it not to be true.

The shaman helps the client enter into a new dream by shifting the meaning of what their hardship represents or symbolizes—this is called shamanic healing. As you learn to think like a shaman, the easier and clearer this process becomes. It doesn't mean that there is no pain in our difficulties, but you learn that the struggles are there to serve you and to direct you, not to punish you. And by giving the difficulties different meaning, they are transformed into power.

I often speak of the "gift in the wound," the hidden offering that lives in our 'eha'eha, or pain and suffering, and reveals itself when we are ready to discover it. For instance, the best healers are the ones who have suffered most, the most empowered women are the ones who have had to fight the hardest for their place at the table, the most visionary innovators are the ones everyone laughed at, and for all of us, the sweetest success comes when we are told—or we tell ourselves—that something can't be done and yet we somehow do it anyway.

Spiritual teacher and author Carolyn Myss has a very simple instruction for living. In a talk based on her book, Sacred Contracts: Awakening Your Divine Potential, she tells us: "Give up the need to understand why things happen as they do, and if the door closes, take the hint." In other words, rather than shake your fist at the sky, protesting the hard knocks that the cards of life have dealt you, begin to wonder why they might be happening for you. If life presents you with a limitation of some kind, assume that it is doing so for a reason that is in your best interest, and adjust accordingly. This isn't just putting a positive spin on things, it's honoring a deeper truth that is the nature of creation itself: "The darkness slips into the light."

Conversely, if there are gifts in the wounds, then there can also be wounds in the gifts. For example, I have seen many clients who developed low self-esteem because, when they were children, their teachers, parents, and authority figures pathologized their spiritual giftedness and high emotional intelligence with a diagnosis of ADHD. These children didn't fit into a standardized curriculum and the established expectations of the community because they were special—not because they were damaged—and their giftedness became a source of pain, rather than one of celebration. As adults, when the hidden truth of their giftedness was finally named as a positive aspect, they were able to create a new sense of who they were.

I remember working with an award-winning television journalist who came from a long line of Harvard intellectuals and luminaries. As a child, she was given love, support, and every possible advantage and opportunity. But despite her success, by the time I met her she was continually plagued with a sense of never feeling good enough. She couldn't understand why she always felt so badly about herself, until she realized that, along with all of her advantages, her parents had set up a subtle competitive dynamic between her and her brothers. When she was finally able see it, she could start to let go of the pressure and judgment that she had always placed on herself.

The darkness slips into light.

The first line of the Kumulipo adds further texture to this discussion of creation: O ke au I kahuli wela ka honua has been translated as, "At a time that turned the heat of the Earth" or "The active seed transforms the Earth with passion." This points toward the hypothesis that there was never an actual beginning to creation, that all creation happens spontaneously of its own accord. It suggests a joyful intention—creation occurring for no other reason than to experience more of itself.

Well, that sounds like love, doesn't it?

The Hawaiians believe that the creative void of the Po is not only the realm of the gods, but also the dwelling place of our Kane, or individual god-self. If this is true, and creation happens all by itself as an act of love, then we can assume love no matter what our experience, because each of us is an individual expression born out of that love. The Hawaiian proverb He punawai kahe wale ke aloha means, "Love is the spring that flows freely," which Serge Kahili King interprets further as "Love is boundless and available to everyone." The shaman trusts in the goodness and rightness of life by seeing it as a creation born of benevolence, inevitability, and a spark of love contained within each of us.

Hawaiian Magic

Historically, magic was a commonplace assumption on the islands of Hawaii. Like all indigenous peoples, the Hawaiians consciously participated in co-creative relationship with the forces of Nature, the universe, and their own minds to effect change and to influence events and circumstances in their physical world. This is called kalakupua, translated as "under control of mysterious or super natural power," or simply as "magic."

From a Huna perspective, magic is our birthright. It is a propensity in all of us that is as natural as any of our five senses, and our bodies and minds are the only tools that we need to practice it. Other than some cultural differences, Huna magic is essentially the same magic that is practiced in the Western Hermetic traditions. Occult associations can make it more complicated (and more loaded) for people than it needs to be, for magic is nothing more than conscious manifestation; the utilization of the natural forces of thought, emotion, energy, and spirit to bring about change. While we have all experienced this to a certain degree, Huna provides a conceptual framework that leads us to understanding and developing the magical resources within.

We have been socialized away from these intrinsic gifts, but to think like a shaman is to return to childlike ways of wonderment and imagination. Like children, shamans play with drums, rattles, and bells; daydream their way into faraway lands; and communicate with their "imaginary friends," the spirits. Shamanism brings us back to a time when we were not victims of the empiricism of science and its postulation that if something can't be measured or explained, it can't be real. Further, many of us rejected the hypocrisy of organized religion and cynically threw the baby out with the bathwater on all things energetic and miraculous, deferring instead to a sterile, scientific view of an entirely mechanical world.

If we are lucky enough to still believe in magic, we are at odds with the judgmental and religious morality that is embedded in the collective unconscious of the West, whether we adhere to it or not. It tells us that we do not deserve to advocate for ourselves magically, and to do so is wrong, egotistical and, in some circles, blasphemous. But it's not just our pulpits of origin that are the problem, we may also have self-limiting stories. These stories often originate in the wounding we received in our families or communities, and continue to disempower us from cultivating our magical gifts.

But from an indigenous perspective, you are here to live your best and most natural life, not the life that looks the most acceptable to your neighbors. Shamans practice magic from a place of deserving-ness and even entitlement. They give themselves full permission to want what they want, to honor their heart's deepest yearnings, and to be unencumbered in their desires' expression. As you will learn, this is what makes our magic most effective—it is the ache of our wanting that seeds kalakupua—our ability to make magic and do wonderous acts as shamans do—into full blossom.

To take this a step further, and I know I'll be ruffling some feath-ers with this one, but here goes: Our primary obligation in this life-time must be to ourselves. This is not selfish. It is centered on the self, yes, but it is not selfish. What is counterintuitive here is that when we focus on ourselves, the entire universe benefits.

The altruistic impulse that many of us have to contribute to human-ity and to the planet happens most effectively when our own needs are met first. Because when they are met, we are able to give from our surplus, rather than from depletion or lack. The more gratitude that we feel in our fullness, the stronger our impulse to share becomes. The instruction that we hear on airplanes to secure your own air mask before helping others with theirs isn't just practical advice, it's sha-manic thinking at its finest.

While the paths of spiritual anorexics, ascetics, martyrs, and bare-foot yogis begging for food are considered legitimate by some in the West, they are, in my opinion, mostly symptomatic of spiritual bypass, or seeking to find spiritual solutions for real-world issues that can only be solved through concrete action. Instead, indigenous wisdom asks us to be in right relationship with the world. This means that we are in a constant cycle of receiving from the Earth, and then giving back to replenish her.

The ancient Hawaiians lived abundantly on their lands; they had a forest of fruit in the morning and an ocean full of fish in the afternoon. They unabashedly and gratefully practiced magic to increase the natural abundance provided throughout their archipelago. By maintaining a deep conversation with the dynamism of Nature and the infinitude of the cosmos, they developed a psychological framework that allowed them to see reality as a matrix of interconnectivity; one that was more energetic than it was material. In doing so, they learned to exist magically. It was this artful connection with life that captured the interest of the early researchers of Huna lore.

Dr. William Tufts Brigham (1841-1926), was an American geologist, ethnologist, and botanist, who lived for many years in Hawaii. As the first curator of Honolulu's Berenice Pauahi Bishop Museum, which holds the largest collection of Polynesian artifacts in the world, from 1892 to 1918, Dr. Brigham spent much of his time researching the Kahunas. While he barely scratched the surface in excavating and understanding the ancient magical practices of the shamans of Hawaii, he was an instrumental player in influencing others to pick up where he left off. One of these was an American novelist and New Age author, Max Freedom Long, who became Brigham's protégé during the later years of Brigham's life, and was a tireless researcher and the author of many books on Huna.

Long's writings on Huna from the earlier part of the twentieth century were clearly influenced by the Theosophical Society and the New Thought movement, but he was among the first to attempt to bring Huna wisdom out of the inland shadows of the secret dwelling places of the Kahunas. Long is a controversial figure, considered an outsider by traditionalists, because he provides us only with his interpretive view of Huna rather than an authentic one. Yet his fascination with

Hawaii, his scholarship with its language, and his earnest yearning to understand the Kahunas cannot be denied.

Brigham made this observation of the mystical powers that he witnessed in the Kahunas, which he shared with Long:

"There is a set of laws for the physical world, and another for the other world. And, try to believe this if you can, but the laws of the other side are so much stronger, that they can be used to neutralize and reverse the laws of the physical."

The magical practices of "the laws of the other side" to which Bishop alludes, and which Long and so many others were to study in depth, send the imagination reeling. There were stories of Pele-worshiping Kahunas who ritualistically walked on lava that had only just cooled and hardened, and was still well above the temperature that could incinerate a man. There was the Love Prayer, hana aloha, which could cause romantic infatuation, and the dark sorcery of the Death Prayer, ana'ana, which could kill another person just by thought—a widely disdained practice considered dangerous for the practitioner. Trafficking in negative energy that extreme could cause illness or misfortune to the practitioner, and there were kahunas who specialized in reversing the ana'ana prayer, sending it back to the very source from which it was sent.

There were also miraculous healings of physical illness through the use of massage (lomi lomi), herbs (pala'au), and prayer (pule), as well as intricate divination systems (hailona) involving casting shells or stones to predict and change the future. It was commonplace for the Hawaiians to have spontaneous visions (akaku) of spiritual beings and to hear supernatural voices (ulaleo). And there were magical practices for fertility, spiritual protection, and harvesting crops, many of which are still in use today.

The Kahunas read omens (ho'ailona) from plants and trees, animal behavior, the stars, and weather systems. Many of them could influence the weather to suit their needs. Certain aspects of the islands are still affiliated with the gods and goddesses traditionally worshipped by the islanders, and these are not symbolic; rather, they are considered to be a direct communion with the gods and goddesses themselves. So to look at the clouds is to behold Lono, the god of agriculture and rain, himself; Pele, the volcano goddess, is the lava; Kane, the god of procreation, makes a visitation in manifest form through the rainbow; and the moon isn't a representation of the moon goddess Hina—rather, when we see the moon, we are actually in Hina's presence.

This immediacy with the metaphysical opened the Hawaiians to messages from the gods (akua) or from the ancestors (aumakua) that offered insights into what time of the day the fish may be at their most plentiful for catching, or from what direction an enemy might attack. If the land and its spirits were able to communicate so effectively, it stood to reason that humans held the same propensity for influencing the outside world. Animism, the idea that everything is alive and conscious, is a cornerstone of shamanic thought. Huna takes it a step further by postulating that everything also wants to connect.

In Hawaiian thought, Mana is the power that can make these connections: aka is the substance through which Mana's powerful influence makes things manifest, and our focused attention, Makia, fuels the process. These were the three factors that Bishop and Long, in their observations of the Kahunas, identified as the building blocks of Hawaiian magic. While Long's work creatively elaborated on what he personally learned from studying the Kahunas, Mana, Aka, and Makia are universally accepted tenets of Hawaiian cosmology.

Mana, Aka, and Makia

Like hula, lanai, tattoo, and mai tai, Mana is one of many Hawaiian words that have made their way into English. It's a difficult word to translate because it has a conceptual difference to anything that is similar to it in the West. Mana has been mistakenly attributed to "life force" and "energy," similar to the chi, ki, and prana of the East, while others think of it as a supernatural force. But Mana is power, pure and simple—a force that effects change. It is an influencing and transforming quality that each of us possess in varying degrees. Mana is the power that creates and it is potential realized.

Humans can cultivate those things that give them Mana by doing anything that would increase health and vitality: eating nutritious food, drinking plenty of water, exercise, deep breathing, positive thinking, telling the truth, spiritual practice, working toward goals, and running lots of love through their systems. The converse is also true. The Kahuna symbol for Mana is water. Max Freedom Long writes:

"Water flows, so does the vital life force. Water fills things, so does the vital life force. Water may leak, so may the life force."

To possess large amounts of Mana, is to become charismatic, a word not often found in books on Shamanism, but an applicable one nonetheless. Charisma is an attractive or alluring personality, but it has a spiritual definition too, "a divinely conferred power or talent to influence," a perfect description of one who is successful in casting spells or making magic. This means that the more Mana we possess, the more charisma; the more charisma: the more influence; the more influence, the more power, and the more power, the stronger our ability to effect change becomes.

Mana, then, as creative power, is the vital force within each of us that makes magic manifest. It is like an electrical current that lives inside you, the source and substance of your personal power, and it is sent out into the world based on the choices that you make about what you want to do with it, with whom you want to share it, who it is that you want to be, and what it is that you want to create. Whether we know it or believe it, we are creating our reality in every moment, and our personal Mana is the activation for that creation.

As I said earlier, Mana can vary in its potency and strength. Long named gradations of this energy on a scale from "basic" to "inspired"

Mana. While purists might scoff at Long's distinctions—Mana is Mana, after all—he identified Mana loa as Mana's highest form. Loa is translated as "great," "tall," and "excessive," and an examination of Mana loa, which I call "divinely inspired Mana" or "grace," elucidates something important about the shaman's mind.

When what we want manifests, when our prayers are answered, when healing occurs, or when energies come together in such a way that feels like Spirit's hand is present, this might be thought of as Mana loa. From the perspective of Universal Shamanism, which seeks to encapsulate the similarities across all indigenous traditions, this harmonious convergence of energies is not the result of spiritual forces outside of us that decide to smile on us and bring us what we want. That would imply that power lies outside of us, which is not a part of Huna philosophy either. Rather, Mana loa, as I have come to understand it experientially, occurs as a reaction to the Mana that we individually possess and "send out" into the world.

The proper mindset behind Huna magic is in the expectation that what we want will most likely come into being when we rid ourselves of all doubt, fear, and shame surrounding our desires, and we cultivate hearts and minds that are in kinship and agreement with what we want. This is why we must legitimize and befriend our wanting and our yearning, because in doing so we align with receiving, and we send out a powerful signal to the universe that contains our innermost essence. What you yearn for is, in fact, a deep part of who you are.

This inner alignment is like the harmonic phenomenon in music called "sympathetic vibration." If you have two identical tuning forks, both tuned to, say, the key of G, and you strike one in close proximity to the other, the unstruck fork will vibrate sympathetically because of its matching harmonic resonance with the other. In Huna, we learn to align our thoughts, beliefs, and attitudes into energetic congruence (sympathetic vibration) with the things that we want to create, and we heal and let go of anything that is out of alignment with them.

This is what makes our magic effective, and it's also what makes us magic prone.

There is a Hawaiian saying, E ku'u Akua e malama au ia oe ma ka no'ono'o, which means, "Oh, my God, let me serve you in thought." The Hawaiians focus on love, beauty and possibility in order to align with the gods, and they do this not just to petition or venerate them, but to become more godlike themselves. In his book Kamalamalama: The Light of Knowledge, Hawaiian author Patrick Ka'ano'i writes,

"In the Hawaiian scheme of life, a god is man, a hereditary ancestor at his best, the supreme excellence of Nature."

Merging our thoughts with the divine requires the radical act of falling madly in love with ourselves, and holding ourselves in the same reverence that we would hold the gods. There is a kind of golden rule on the islands which can be translated as, E aloha ia 'oe iho me like aloha 'oe ia Ke Akua Nui: "To love yourself as you love God." To do this would be an entirely different way of thinking for most of us, and to honor and cultivate this divinity within is to bring our personal Mana into harmonic resonance with the Mana loa, or the gifts of the omnipotent.

This brings us to a foundational concept of earth-based spirituality and thought, one that is almost impossible to fathom—we are not beings who need exist in helpless reactivity to the spiritual forces of the universe, powerless nothings blown around by the all-powerful winds of creation. Rather, we are the primary cause of the creative force of our lives, and the spiritual intelligences of the universe follow our lead. We hold directive power in how they relate to us, because the way in which we organize our thoughts, beliefs, and intentions indicate to them how they can best show up for us and *what we are willing to receive.*

The first lines of a famous Hawaiian chant are, E iho ana o luna, E pi'i ana o lalo, which translates as, "That which is above shall come down, that which is below shall rise up." While this chant was originally a call for Hawaiian strength and sovereignty, it also has an esoteric meaning which echoes the classic spiritual adages "As above, so below," and "As within, so without." According to Huna, there is nothing outside of us or beyond our influence, and we can learn to use the power within us, our Mana, to "rise up" to the gods, and find that they reflexively "come down" to meet us, wherever we happen to be.

If our infinitely improvable Mana can resonate with the power of gods and beyond, and even reach them directly, how does it get there? Long and Brigham said that the force that makes magic needs a substance through which it can act, and that substance is aka. Aka is a testament to the genius of the ancient Hawaiians because they identified something that, centuries later, would become a basic tenet of quantum theory and mechanics: There is no such thing as empty space.

Aka is translated as "shadow," "essence," "an embryo at the moment of conception," and "the faint glimmer preceding the rising of the moon." In other words, it isn't the thing itself, it's the substance of the thing. To break down the word further shows aka as a means for connection: The syllable a means "to direct" and ka means "to send out on a vine." As the combination of these two words, aka signifies the field of potential in and around everything that carries and conducts energy and thought.

Other Earth-based spiritual traditions call this element ether, or the fifth element—the immanence that allows everything in the universe to connect with everything else, and through that connection, to create anew. A literal translation of aka is "a sticky substance," and what sticks to it is consciousness. Aka isn't consciousness, it's the potential for consciousness, and the vast aka field, with its limitless cords or tendrils of connection, "lights up" as consciousness and power pass through it. This is mirrored in modern physics' string theory, a theoretical framework in which creation is made up of connective strings of subatomic substance.

Aka is analogous to radio or satellite frequencies that we can't see, but which we know are there. These frequencies exist in the atmosphere and all around us, and we tune in to them by turning on a receiver. Everyone on the planet who has a cellphone theoretically has the potential to reach you, but it is only those who actually know and dial your number who do. Likewise, while aka is the raw material that makes up the universe and our attention, even a mere thought is enough to begin the process of sending out its vines of connection. The consistency of our focus and the level of our emotional investment, which helps to increase our focus even more, strengthens it into a fuller realization.

We experience interconnective aka whenever we think of someone and immediately receive an email or a text message from them, when we feel that we are being watched only to turn our head and find someone staring, or when we dream about an event that ends up happening sometime in the future. For me, the consistent and repeated focus that I have had on Hawaii and Shamanism has created a powerful aka connection that has actualized into Mana in the form of the book that you now hold in your hands.

There may be no aka connection between you and, say, Lake Natron in Tanzania, or with Takeru Kobyashi, the world-record-breaking hotdog eater from Japan (although there is now, I'm afraid), but you probably have a very strong and dynamic aka connection to a parent, a child, a political party, or your life's work—and the result of this connection is the creative influence, or Mana, that you have on them.

I spoke earlier about cultivating that which gives us Mana that is powerful enough to be in energetic resonance with the gods. Because aka is the shadowy substance of unrealized potential that can connect with and become anything that our intent and imagination might conceive, we can transform into the highest expression of ourselves simply by lending the light of our awareness to whatever within us may be tacit or undeveloped. The Hawaiian word for god or goddess is akua, so only one letter differentiates the vast distance from the embryonic essence of aka to the supremely realized state of akua.

Finally, power (Mana) and potential (aka) need consistent attention and focus in order to actualize. This brings us to the final aspect of the triumvirate recipe for Huna magic: Makia, translated as "to concentrate" or "to aim or strive." The requisite force that fuels our creative intentions into manifestation is our ability to direct our consciousness with focused consistency—and Makia, or "aimed thought," is that potent force. The importance of Makia can't be overemphasized, because it is the cornerstone concept of the Huna system: "Everything that exists is created by our thoughts."

The Hawaiian language is loaded with words indicating the power of the mind. For instance, mana'o means "thought." Since Mana means "creative power" and o means "here," hence, mana'o means "power is here in thought." Mana'o'i'o is translated as "to have faith or confidence" or "to believe." This word breaks down into mana and i'o, which means "true" or "real," which we can synthesize into "the power of thought makes things real."

The human body is called kino, which contains the kaona, or hidden meaning, "a highly energized thought form." There is a Hawaiian proverb that says, Ke kino ka hale no ka mana'o, which means, "The body is the house for the thoughts." In other words, the body itself is formed of thoughts and so is the entire corporeal world in which the body exists. And, to bring this point fully home, the word akua, which we've seen means "god or goddess," has another meaning: "a fully formed idea in action." In other words, a god is nothing more than the full realization of a consciousness that we can create inside our own heads.

As you can see, magic is made possible through the hidden universe of the shaman's mind. Shamans consciously create effectively because they tend and harvest their personal power (Mana), they discipline and fine-tune their thinking (Makia), and they never forget that infinite potential exists absolutely everywhere (aka).

This foray into Hawaiian cosmology demonstrates that an entirely different belief system emerges from cultivating a mind that assumes the miraculous and seeks to create it, always entertains possibility, remains forever curious about every experience, and builds up the dynamism of the self. Huna, as you'll see, doesn't dictate what our beliefs should be; it's an ingenious invitation to help you create the ones that work best for you, enabling you to create your own unique brand of magic-making and grow your shaman's mind from its aka to its akua.

CHAPTER THREE

HUNA BASICS

Huna

To some, Huna is the name of the esoteric and spiritual philosophy of Hawaii. The Hawaiian elder Nelita Anderson has said that traditional Hawaiian spirituality was never actually given a name, and if one were to be used, the most appropriate one would probably be *Ho'omana*–originating from the words *Ho'o*, "to make," and *Mana*, "power." Huna and Ho'omana are often used interchangeably, despite the fact that among them there are innumerable variations from a host of different local, religious, and family traditions.

There has been a small movement to delegitimize the word Huna entirely, in order to discredit Max Freedom Long, who used it as the title of his system, which was based on the knowledge of the Kahunas he studied but also included many of his own ideas. Others cry foul when any non-Hawaiian teaches or writes about Hawaiian spirituality in any capacity. Serge Kahili King has said that he sometimes regrets choosing the word Huna to name the specific knowledge passed down to him by his adoptive Hawaiian family because he is not Hawaiian by blood and his family lineage is not connected to Max Long.

As I have mentioned, there is no such thing as one definitive Hawaiian spirituality, but the effectiveness of Huna—and its numerous cross-cultural correspondences with other indigenous, philosophical, and spiritual traditions—cannot be denied. While much of the Huna that I share in this book comes from the Kahili family tradition, it is not an unequivocal representation—nor am I entirely sure that Serge Kahili King would agree with of all of it. A handful of other teachers and authors, such as Dr. Ihaleakala Hew Len and Morrnah Simeona, have also been influences, and I've peppered my writing with my own interpretations of this material.

Shamanism and spiritual preciousness don't make good bedfellows. Some contemporary seekers spend too much time and energy on semantics, and/or are judgmental of spiritual perspectives other than their own, missing entirely their overarching similarities. Others resist the contemporary spiritual phenomenon that the late Kahuna Hale Kealohalani Makua called the New World Religion—an interspiritual fusion of all of the faith traditions coming together into a unified whole.

The fact is, each of us is now being asked to be part of a global effort to effect real change on the planet—and, frankly, *we need to get on with it.* The gods want us to be well yesterday so that we can best help with this sacred work. Rather than engaging in further debate about what esoteric Hawaiian wisdom should be called, I defer to Serge Kahili King's late uncle, one of his main teachers, who told him, "The knowledge is the knowledge, whatever you want to call it."

That being said, my position is that Huna is a perfect name for this knowledge because it is loaded with meanings that help us understand how to use it and what it can do. Like many mystery school traditions that have found their way into the mainstream over the last fifty years, Huna is sometimes thought of as a secret wisdom, and one of its translations in Hawaiian is, "hidden secret." But Huna is not meant to be withheld or concealed; it is also defined as "minute particle," "minutia," and "powdery," which indicates more precisely that Huna wisdom is analogous to dust, mist, or fine sea spray. *Huna is something that is difficult to see, something that is definitely there, but not obvious.*

The word Huna has additional hidden meanings (or *kaona* in Hawaiian) that are roughly synonymous with the Chinese concept of yin and yang, the symbol of duality and the balance of opposing forces that exist in all things (black/white, back/front, life/death, sky/earth). The syllables *hu* and *na* are equivalent to the contrary, yet unifying polarities of yang and yin: *Hu* is the masculine, active principle, translated as "to rise or swell," "to percolate," and "to surge or rise to the surface"; *na* means "calmed," "pacified," or "soothed," signifying a receptive, feminine aspect.

Huna can be thought of metaphorically, like a wave in the ocean that progresses through movement (hu) and release (na). The wave surges upward, leading to resistance and a buildup of stress, until it crests downward into release and resolution—and then the process begins anew. Most of the time, when healing is needed, we find ourselves "stuck" at a stress point at the top or bottom of the wave. Remember that the root of all disease, or what the Hawaiians call *ma'i*, is tension, and *ola*, "health," or "a state of being healed" is created through the release of tension. And to facilitate that release we may sometimes need more hu (action), while at other times, more na (stillness) is called for.

To put it all together, the shaman uses Huna wisdom to tap into difficult-to-see realities in order to find and restore the unity and balance that inherently exists within them, and healing is brought to any conflict or incongruence through a process of action or release. This happens in large part by a change in thinking. Huna has such potency because it implies that the hidden truth in everything is harmony—embedded in every problem is its solution, and a means to that solution. The shaman operates under the assumption that *the healing that he or she seeks is already there.*

If this all seems a little "out there," welcome to Shamanism, and Aloha to Huna! Developing a shaman's mind requires that you finetune your inner vision toward peripheral truths; develop a paradoxical curiosity that searches for power where it doesn't at first seem to reside; become laser-focused on your mental attitudes, habits, and beliefs; and believe that the right solutions can't help but reveal themselves.

About ninety-five percent of the people who come to me with a specific problem have either identified the wrong one or are enmeshed in a story and belief system that won't allow that particular problem to be solved. The shaman's mind doesn't resonate with limitation because, as Huna holds, limitation is not the nature of reality. Powerlessness is even more uninteresting, because to think like a shaman is to know that, for every problem, there is *always* something that can be done. With wisdom, attention, focus, love, presence, power, and flexibility, the shaman knows that absolutely anything is possible.

No problem can exist or would ever have been created if the person with the problem had known that:

1. They created it with their thoughts and beliefs.
2. They are inextricably connected to every solution for it in the entire universe.
3. They can create something different by focusing on something different.
4. They can do so right now in the present moment.
5. They can choose the most loving solution.
6. They have infinite power within themselves to create to do so.
7. They can try something else if what they attempt doesn't work.

These are, of course, simply restatements of the Seven Principles of Huna, and each one will be addressed in great detail later in this book. At this point, the most important thing is to continue to feel into the unique quality of the shaman's mind, for the more you can understand how a shaman thinks, the better you can follow the shaman's example and allow potentiality, healing, and purpose to guide you in all that you do.

The Kahuna

If Huna is the esoteric knowledge of Hawaii, then the Kahuna is the master teacher and practitioner of it, right? Well, sort of. Previously, I have used the terms "shaman" and "Kahuna" interchangeably, but while they essentially mean the same thing, my use of "Kahuna" has been one of convenience, though slightly incorrect. Often translated as "priest," "wizard," or "minister," the more precise meaning of "Kahuna" is actually "an expert in any profession" or "an authority of some aspect of Hawaiian culture."

When seekers come to Hawaii looking for a Kahuna, the question they need to answer is: "What kind of Kahuna are you looking for?" The word Kahuna needs additional words to qualify it. A master shaman, the kind that we aspire to be, would be a *Kahuna Kupua*. You would go to a *Kahuna Kaukaukalolo* to receive an expert tattoo. A *Kahuna Lapaʻau* is a master herbalist and accomplished medicinal healer. A *Kahuna Kalaiwaʻa* would teach you how to build a canoe, and a *Kahuna Kumu Hula* would be your hula instructor. If you wanted to meet the "Big Kahuna" on the beach, like in the '60s surfer comedies, you would look for the expert surfer, *Kahuna nui heʻe nalu*, the "best wave-slider." (By the way, the real Hawaiian Big Kahunas are usually far better looking than the ones from the movies!)

Traditionally, there were three "types" of Kahunas: those whose expertise centered around the physical body such as bodywork, war, or athletics; those more connected to intellectual pursuits like astronomy, herbalism, or psychology; and, finally, those schooled in the spiritual realms of divination, prayer, and magic. But, regardless of one's field of expertise, the body, mind, and spirit are always inseparable, and it is the *Kahuna Kupua*, or shaman, whose work it is to help facilitate the integration of all three.

The Kahuna Kapua, or any traditional shaman, creates correction and wellbeing by restoring things to rightness, and by healing the relationships that we have with our mind and our body, with ourselves and others, with others and others and, finally, with everyone and the planet. The Hawaiians have a term for this balanced state of equanimity, *pono*, which means, "goodness," "rightness," and "true condition of Nature" It is related to ho'oponopono, the practice that seeks to correct things or to make things right through forgiveness and love, and as the repetition of the word *pono* suggests, to make them doubly so.

The shaman is part healer of the body, part psychotherapist, and part spiritualist, and it is in the combination of these roles that he or she steps into the ultimate role of steward for the Earth. For it is the life's work of the shaman—or, as the Hawaiians would say, the shaman's *kuleana*, or responsibility—to make things pono, one being at a time. That is the shaman's required contribution to all sentient life, to the living planet, and ultimately to the one universe. The Hawaiians have a specific phrase that they use to express their love for their islands: *Malama ka 'aina*, which means, "To care for and protect the land as you would a sibling or parent." To do this most effectively, the shaman must include the preservation and support of all the sentient beings who live on that land.

At the beginning of this book, I asked you to remember, reinvigorate, or begin to discover what your contribution to the world might be, and how your life might serve the collective. To be a Kahuna Kapua or a shaman—or at least to learn to think like one—it is vital that you identify this purpose because, to the shaman, *nothing else matters*. Making a difference, leaving the world a better place than you found it, taking care of others, celebrating life, and delighting in the wellbeing of the community—these are all of the factors that propel the shaman into action.

I once had a colleague, a medical sleep specialist, who told me that the most effective way to treat sleep disorders is for the patient to identify their own life's purpose—how their existence serves the collective—and align with it in action. Similarly, your shaman's mind will grow exponentially when you organize your life around how you intend to influence and serve the world, and then insist that every choice and action that you take contributes to this intention.

(I just said a mouthful, so you may want to read that last paragraph again!)

The title of shaman, or Kahuna Kapua, is actually not something that one chooses for oneself; rather, one is *named* this because one's very presence indicates that this is who one is. It is a title of recognition given by the community based on the way in which they witness how a certain individual shows up in the world. It is, indeed, a rare and special person who is called to a position of leadership whose sole purpose is to remind everyone that they are God, and that they already live in heaven, and to help them make things pono when, for whatever reason, they may have forgotten it.

To paraphrase one of the Huna principles, *the world reflects back to you your innermost essence.* If you want to merge with the mind of the shaman, attuning your loving intentions toward our shared world is tantamount to your success; when you are in this frame of mind, the gods can most easily reach you and support you, because that is what they are doing too.

Huna Origins: The Ancient Pacific Continent of Mu

Having worked and studied with shamans in North, Central, and South America as well as the Far East, I have observed that they adhere to surprisingly similar practices, values, and worldviews. They are earthy people who allow their hearts, their connection to spirit, and their attunement to Nature to guide them in their lives. While they are often highly intelligent, they aren't generally heady or ana-lytical thinkers, and while they can often seem quite fierce, they are for the most part gentle, reverent, and humble.

The indigenous wisdom of the shaman comes from a place of deep internal knowing—it's an oral tradition that is passed down by elders, transmitted through bloodlines, and is very much influenced by observing the Earth's natural cycles. The shaman's ways are so ingrained and integrated that many shamans seem to care little about consciously understanding why they do what they do, or even exactly how they do it. This is why it can be difficult to understand them, and challenging for them to teach Western students.

Shamans have their own unique logic, a way of seeing the world that is cultural, metaphysical, and local. How does one convey a way of being to those who may have an entirely different perception of real-ity? Unlike so many of us in the West, shamanic people have generally not spent their lives striving for a "better way," so they don't have that "seeker" context, and, traditionally (at least until recent years), they have not have the specific intention of teaching outsiders. All of these factors make insight into their internal process elusive and can create difficulties in their ability to convey their wisdom to others.

When contemporary students study Shamanism, they are often guided toward the experience of it, rather than to trying to under-stand it intellectually. After all, there are no definitive shamanic man-ifestos, sets of scriptures, or lists of commandments to follow. Because we have so little to go on, learning how a shaman thinks is only pos-sible through the inferences that we can make by observing them, rather than by employing theoretical or philosophical constructs that could ground the Western mind in a deeper understanding.

We are not, however, without some guidance. The gods wanted shamanic knowledge preserved, and they wanted it to be available to those who were ready to use it, so we find that at least some of these answers are buried deep underneath the Hawaiian Islands. There are many myths, legends, and even channeled pieces of information about the ancient civilization of the lost continent of *Mu* in the South Pacific, which is where many believe Huna had its origins.

Mu, or *Lemuria*, as it is sometimes called by non-Hawaiians, is said to have existed at a time of the "early earth," a huge land mass where Hawaii now stands. Its inhabitants were said to be an advanced "star people" who came from the Pleiades. Some Hawaiians today say that they are descendants of the *menehune*, the people of the secret power, or the people of Mu, who are known as the "wee folk"—gnome-like beings who are still believed to mischievously haunt the islands at night. In fact, it's said that if you focus your gaze in just the right way over the expanse of what the Hawaiians might call the "Hawaiian Ocean," and it's sometimes possible to catch a misty glimpse of the phantom islands, where the Menehune are still believed to live.

The people of Mu were considered spiritually gifted, and are at least partially responsible for teaching and spreading esoteric wisdom throughout the world. According to Diane Stein, author of *Essential Reiki*, the study of Reiki was part of the curriculum in Mu children's education. Other versions of the Mu legend hypothesize that this ancient continent wasn't the source of knowledge itself, but was rather the recipient of powerful spiritual influences from the Far East, the Americas, Oceania, and Africa.

It has been further theorized that when cataclysmic shifts in the Earth plunged the continent of Mu underneath the sea, not all of its inhabitants perished, and a handful survived to pass on the ancient ways to future generations. Thousands of years later, during the period between 325 and 1250 A.D., many worldwide populations still felt the influence of Mu, and lived in harmony and balance by practicing Huna or something quite similar, like Wicca and Tantra, until these "balanced systems" came under attack by the male-dominated, patriarchal cultures of the time.

Most importantly, the people of Mu took it upon themselves to create a language that would help preserve their knowledge. Today, some consider Polynesian to be that language, and linguists have found etymological correspondences in the languages of other cultures located continents away.

Now, I have absolutely no proof that anything I have just stated is entirely true—at least in the consensus reality that we all are agreeing to at the moment. But, to be honest, I don't really care, as long as it stirs your imagination. It is certainly unmistakable that Hawaii sits on a vortex of spiritual power, and it is abundantly clear that much of what Huna philosophy espouses is found at least partially in a host of other spiritual technologies.

What I can say for certain is that in addition to the secret wisdom that was passed down orally by the native Hawaiian elders and wisdom-keepers, and held deeply within the energy of the islands themselves, the Hawaiian language is a primary source of Huna knowledge.

Seven Hawaiian words—*'Ike, Kala, Makia, Manawa, Aloha, Mana,* and *Pono*—became the seeds for the seven Huna principles that are unique translations of these words by Serge Kahili King, and they, more than anything else that I have ever encountered in all my shamanic travels, allow us the easiest entry into the shaman's mind.

PART TWO

The SEVEN PRINCIPLES of HUNA

One of the most exciting aspects of Huna is its ability to be blended with and practically applied to contemporary cultural paradigms, modern conceptions of the self, and many other spiritual systems. As we explore the seven Huna principles, I reiterate that, wherever you happen to reside, our purpose here is to bring this material from the Hawaiian Islands to your individual psyches and hearts in practical and usable ways.

So far, we have utilized Hawaiian concepts, traditions, and history as springboards into universal indigenous thought. You will find that studying the Huna principles deepens this understanding by providing a philosophical, shamanic framework for successful living that has resonance and relevance far beyond the South Pacific.

CHAPTER FOUR

THE WORLD IS WHAT
YOU THINK IT IS

Ike: To see, to know, to recognize, to perceive, to experience, to be aware.

Years ago, I took a meditation training with a rather spicy Buddhist nun. At a certain point in the class, she announced to everyone in the room, "*You know what? None of you know absolutely anything about anything!*" Now, she wasn't trying to insult her students, she was telling us that we were completely unaware of the assumptions, expectations, and beliefs that we held, and that we had no idea of how the content of our minds was creating limitations in our experience. This is the essence of the first principle of Huna, which says the world is, becomes, and reflects back what goes on inside your head: *The world is what you think it is.*

This principle doesn't just say that the way you think about the world will reflect your personal experience of it. It's also stating that the world itself will energetically and physically shift, based on how you think about it. In other words, you are in a co-creative relationship with the world, and it creates itself as a reflection of your very thoughts. We now know, thanks to the experiments of Japanese author Masaru Emoto, that human consciousness has an effect on the molecular structure of water, and similar studies have demonstrated the "observer effect" of Quantum Mechanics: Just as humans are physiologically affected by their environment and what they observe in it, so too are the objects of observation and their environment affected by the observer.

An experiment that recently took the internet by storm exemplifies Huna's first principle. In this experiment, two identical houseplants were placed next to each other in the hallway of an elementary school. The students were instructed to treat one plant as "popular," thinking positive thoughts about it and saying kind and reassuring things to it, and to "bully" the other plant by thinking negatively about it and saying threatening, demeaning things to it. Meanwhile, each plant was cared for and watered in the same way, and was not touched by the students. Over a period of weeks, the "popular" plant thrived and grew, while the "bullied" one yellowed and wilted. It is also noteworthy that not only did the plants change their forms, but so did the children, as they used their thoughts and intentions to "become" the meanness of the bully or the kindness of the admirer.

Everything has a consciousness, everything is alive and responsive, and everything wants to connect. If that is true, then it stands to reason that everything also has the capacity to relate to our thoughts. Shamans, with their natural, animistic outlook, have always known this—and now, so do you. And when I say "everything," I mean *literally everything*—your car, your liver, the room you're in, raindrops, the ocean, cough medicine, wind, and this book. If you try to connect with any of these as if they were alive and responsive, you will see that they start to relate to you differently as well.

I have such an intimate relationship with a few rocks who live at my office that I would be beside myself with grief if something were to happen to them, and I am fairly certain that they feel the same way about me. Because I know that everything can respond to my thoughts, you can bet that, as a nervous flier, whenever I board a plane I make a point of saying hello to it, and offering a few words of encouragement. And, by the way, if you want to decide that everything isn't alive and responsive, doesn't have a consciousness, and can't connect with you, then so be it, and that will be your experience: The world is what *you* think it is.

We create our reality with our thoughts, and reality creates itself based on them as well. This means that what we think and believe can't *not* become our world, because our world is nothing more than a result of the dream that we are dreaming in every moment, through the thoughts we think and the beliefs we choose. To see reality as a dream that we create moment by moment is to see through the eyes of the shaman's mind. For all intents and purposes, thoughts and beliefs are synonymous, because our thoughts create our beliefs, and our beliefs, in turn, create the context of our thoughts. Or, to put it another way, how we see life is what we believe about it, and what we believe is how we see life. Therefore, what we create is limited only by our imagination, because we can overcome any limitation by simply thinking something else.

A highly ingenious—and ultimately insidious—spinning of the first Huna principle was exemplified in 2017 when the people of the United States were introduced to the existence of "alternative facts," and were told over and over by a certain presidential administration that the entirety of the mainstream news media and most of what they reported was "fake." The promulgators of this political phenomenon essentially told the American people, *"The world is what you think it is, and we want you to think such and such."* It is more than surprising— though not really, given the first principle of Huna—to realize that it worked. A new "reality" was created for millions of people who chose to accept a different set of "facts." The alternative news outlets that supported these alternative facts flourished, and small, seemingly evidentiary changes occurred that made at least some of these false facts partially "true." This was a mass shift in reality, and millions chose to participate. The world was what they all thought it was.

While this example is actually a negative application of Huna's first principle, it also speaks to Huna's potency. Just imagine it being put to use in ways that are expansive, encouraging of growth, and loving. *What we think is so, is so.* How we see the world determines our experience of it. Knowing that your mind holds such creative power, you must—if you want to—start paying meticulous attention to the thoughts and beliefs to which you give legitimacy and clout, and reexamine and change the ones that aren't getting you where you want to go—or, rather, aren't creating the world that you want.

If you believe that you are only supposed to exist for others, your life will be filled with those who will take from you. If, as a single woman over thirty-five, you believe that all women over thirty-five will end up alone, you will probably have that experience. If you believe that you are unlovable, a satisfying love life will likely be elusive. If you believe there is no God, then God won't have much presence in your life.

Conversely, if you believe that a walk in the forest will help you find an answer to an important question, the forest will start talking to you when you take that walk. If you believe that you will always have abundant finances, money will tend to flow. If you believe that the perfect job is out there, just waiting for you, you'll be more likely to find it. If you believe that the world is what you think it is, then you are probably going to prioritize positive mind-states, self-love, and expansive belief systems.

Now, I know what you might be thinking: "I've read this far into this book, and this guy is telling me I co-create my reality? I know this already. I've heard it before. I even believe it!" Well, yes, but do you *really* believe it? Do you believe it all of the time or do you just selectively believe it about certain things when it suits you? Are all parts of you on board with this, or do you have doubts? Is it a consistent practice for you to see the world, and your role in creating it, in this way, or is it only something that you remember when you really want something, or when you are being consciously "spiritual"? Are there certain relationships or habits in your life that make you want to avoid looking at how your thoughts and beliefs have created them? Are there beliefs that you know you should examine or change, but that you resist because you actually don't want to change—or because the necessary change would be painful, scary, or invasive?

I don't mean to be a poison pill here; I am simply offering you the gentle instruction that this principle (along with the other six) requires a commitment of consistent adherence, and sometimes brutal honesty, in order for it to be effective. According to Huna, mixed thinking gets mixed results. As I mentioned earlier, a shaman's wisdom comes from a place of deep knowing; absolutely ingrained in the shaman's fundamental outlook is the knowledge that one's thoughts create one's world—not just some thoughts some of the time, but all thoughts, in every instant.

Accepting that the outer world reflects back your inner world can be difficult. Many times during my workshops or trainings someone has asked me if I am implying that they created their own illness or some other difficult life situation. There are no easy answers to such questions, in part because we may not know what we actually believe, or our beliefs may be so unconscious that we aren't even aware of them. Likewise, we may have longstanding wounding that has caused negative mental habits and self-limiting stories that contaminate our thoughts.

But, according to Huna, you have some degree of complicity with everything that happens to you and everything that you experience, although that doesn't necessarily mean that you have done anything intentionally. When we examine difficulties in our lives, and seek to understand our part in their creation, we might need to widen the lens to provide a larger perspective that includes the lessons of the soul. At other times, we may simply have to defer to the Great Mystery. However, if you take responsibility for your causative involvement in the creation of your world, the more empowered you will become, and the more choices will be made available to you.

Many years ago, I was evicted from a New York City apartment because I advertised it on one of those online, vacation rental websites to be rented when I was going to be out of town. My apartment had only been listed for a few days before I learned that by advertising it online, I had unknowingly broken the terms of my lease. I promptly deleted the advertisement, although the landlord, unbeknownst to me, had already seen it. What followed was a year of court battles, headaches, and major expense, and despite the fact that it had only been listed online for a few days, and I didn't actually rent it to anyone, the landlord eventually threw me out.

Afterward, as I soul-searched (and whined to whoever would listen) about how a model tenant such as myself could make just one innocent mistake and yet be treated so unfairly, I was hit square in the gut with the real truth: I had always had major fears about money, which was why I had listed my apartment on that vacation rental website in the first place. Had I really needed to jeopardize my living space just to make a few hundred extra dollars while I was out of town for a couple of weeks? The world reflected back my scarcity thinking about money by making my life financially scarce. It was difficult for me to learn that I had actually created this hardship for myself, and that my money issues were so ingrained that I was hardly aware of just how strong they were. But once I saw my part in the creation of this unfortunate situation, I used it to begin to examine and address my negative beliefs and fears around finances.

If our thoughts have so much power, then figuring out how and what we think seems like a pretty major priority. While I definitely believe in the benefits of psychotherapy, I also believe that you don't necessarily need to hire an "expert" to help you understand the content of your unconscious beliefs and your habitual thinking. The easiest and most immediate way to do this is simply *to look at your life*. Your relationships, finances, career, health, home, and spiritual connection are going to tell you everything that you need to know, because each one is a representation of how you see the world and yourself in relation to it.

And listen up now: If there is anything about your life that you don't like, it is safe to say that you have beliefs (unconscious or not) that indicate that *it's perfectly okay with you that certain things are not okay*.

The good news is that in order to make this principle work for you, you have the power to take one hundred percent responsibility for yourself, while the bad news is that you need to take one hundred percent responsibility for yourself, because this principle doesn't let you off the hook. You get to decide what you want your experience to be, and when, for whatever reason, things don't go your way, you get to decide how you want to think about that too. Whatever you end up deciding will always have validity because the world is what you think it is, and you can make it be whatever you want it to be. In Huna, we consider a key *Kupua* (magical) power to be *choice*, and implied in the principle of Ike is that *you always get to choose*.

If change is as easy as thinking differently, then why is change so difficult? Because changing your thinking requires diligence. When you choose to align your beliefs with what you want, internal fears and doubts will inevitably present themselves and try to undermine or block your efforts. You'll need to support the choice to change your mind with actionable steps that will help you validate your new beliefs and employ a consistency of attention in order to habituate them (which will be discussed in greater detail when we get to third principle). It can absolutely be done, but it takes work.

When we have difficulty choosing beliefs and thoughts that lead to our own growth and potential, there are likely to be unresolved issues from the past that still have not been healed. If this resonates for you, then you can give a gift to yourself (and to the world) by working with someone who can support you in addressing it. If you are unsure of what beliefs to create, choose those that make you feel happy, hopeful, empowered, and excited, and avoid any that make you feel limited, shameful, afraid, or tired. It is really that simple. But simplicity does not necessarily mean ease, because if the activation of positive beliefs feels foreign to you, then you are probably going to have to do serious battle with some longstanding habits and storylines of negativity, shame, and fear. It takes vigilant action on your part to become aware of what you believe, and to choose over and over again to believe something else that is more beneficial.

I was once asked, "In your experience, what does 'healed' look like?" My response was: *"'Healed' is when we have set up our lives in such a way that we are enjoying the moment most of time."* This is what I am inviting you to do for yourself. The quality of what goes on between your ears is vitally important because the world is either blessed or stuck with whatever you decide to create there.

Ike Practice — Beliefs

If the world is what you think it is, then we need to begin to examine exactly what we are thinking and what we are believing. Journaling is a great practice for this because it requires us to slow down enough to attend to our internal experience and build a deeper rapport with ourselves.

Take plenty of time with the following exercise. Read through it until you fully grasp it, and then carve out some time to write it out. By becoming aware of our habits of thought, we can effect great change and influence over our lives.

Beliefs Exercise

*In a journal, make a list of at least twenty negative, core beliefs that you
have about yourself and the world. These are the fixed negativities that
you feel are true, more often than not, about you and your life. Really
go to town here; let all that negativity and limitation flow as you write
them all down.*

Examples of negative core beliefs about yourself might be:

✓ *I hate my body.*

✓ *I'll never be thin.*

✓ *I'm not smart.*

✓ *I'm a bad person/mother/father/daughter/son/sibling.*

✓ *I'm going to die young.*

✓ *I'll never have money.*

✓ *I'll never be a teacher/singer/actor/astronaut.*

✓ *I'm afraid to speak in public.*

✓ *I'm ugly.*

✓ *I'll be alone forever.*

✓ *I always attract bad boys/narcissists/addicts.*

✓ *I am always expected to give, but I never receive.*

✓ *I don't know who I am.*

✓ *I'm sexually dysfunctional.*

✓ *I'll never find love.*

Examples of negative core beliefs about the world might be:

✓ *All men are ...*

✓ *All women are ...*

✓ *All people are ....*

✓ *All women over forty are ....*

✓ *Money is ....*

✓ *Life is unfair.*

✓ *People are inherently cruel/uncaring/backstabbing.*

✓ *There is no God.*

✓ *Faith is useless.*

✓ *[Such and such] hasn't happened for me yet, so I assume that it never will.*

Now, take some time to rewrite each negative belief as its opposite and positive aspect—even if you don't believe it or can't imagine it ever to be true. Use your creativity, and spin each negative belief into one that is filled with potential, possibility, hope, and inspiration. This can be as simple as changing "I am ugly" to "I am beautiful," or "I will always be alone" to "The perfect mate is on his way."

You may choose to "argue" with your negative belief. For example, if your negative belief is "I will never have a relationship," you can try something like: "Are you trying to tell me that you are some kind of fortuneteller who knows that I will always be alone forever, that there is no one in the entire universe for me, that you have some superpower that knows everything about everything?"

If you get stuck with the rewriting from negative to positive, or you can't possibly imagine a new positive belief ever being true for you, the following language can help: "I am in the process of ...." Or: "I am looking forward to ...." For example, "I am in the process of knowing that I am beautiful." And "I am looking forward to the romance that is coming into my life."

Once you have created your new, positive list of beliefs, spend some time with it. Keep a copy in your wallet or your purse, around your house or in your workspace—or, even better, in all of these places. Dwell on your new beliefs, get very familiar with them, and think about them frequently. Begin to recognize (and seek out) other people who appear to think and believe in the new ways that you aspire to, and do your best to avoid the people who don't. You may even find inspiration in fictional characters from books or movies who seem to embody your new positive beliefs. Most importantly, pay meticulous attention to the negative beliefs as they come into your consciousness. When they do, replace *them immediately with the new ones. Do this over and over again, until they start to stick.*

Determine and take specific action steps to help solidify and strengthen your new beliefs. If your new belief is around a career change, is there a class or training that you need to take, and are you signed up? If you are renegotiating your beliefs about your romantic life, have you gotten on that dating website? Have you started the exercise program that will make you feel more beautiful or connected to your body? Did you purchase those new art supplies? Have you started that new meditation practice? Are you seeking out that new therapist or healer? Have you ended that relationship? Did you listen to that podcast?

And, in each case, if your answer is no or "not yet," ask yourself, "Why not? What is the belief that is getting in my way?"

Once you have been through this process, you will have learned much about where you are, where you want to go, and what you are up against. Developing a shaman's mind is a lifelong endeavor, and changing beliefs or adjusting thinking won't happen overnight, but they absolutely will happen.

You are learning to create reality with your thoughts. With the beauty and majesty of Hawaii as an aspirational ideal, that reality can be as sumptuous as you would ever want it to be—one that, as the next principle, Kala (pronounced *kah-lah*), states, is limited only by the restrictions your own inspired vision, heart, and ingenuity may conceive.

CHAPTER FIVE

THERE ARE NO LIMITS

Kala: To loosen, untie, free, release, unburden, let go, undo.

A few times a year, on a remote beach called Playa Ostional near Nosara, Costa Rica, a remarkable event called "the *arribada*," meaning "the arrival" in Spanish, takes place. Over a period of a few days, hundreds of thousands of Olive Ridley Sea Turtles return to the beach of their birth, just as their parents did decades earlier, to lay and bury their eggs, continuing the cycle of life. Some of these turtles have been tagged and studied by oceanographers, and despite having traveled in the open sea to places as far away as India, they always eventually make the great journey back to this same small Central American beach, with many of them not having previously returned there since the day that they were born and began swimming.

Turtles have limited vision, and it has been theorized by scientists that they navigate the vast ocean by observing the sun and stars, by feeling into the Earth's electromagnetic fields, and by connecting with the ocean currents. Just prior to their massive emergence onto the beach, under the cover of night, and in conjunction with the moon cycles and its effect on the tides that the turtles ride into shore, thousands of them gather in huge groups called "flotillas."

On what scientists have only been able to describe as "some secret signal," they arrive in such great numbers that any predators who might otherwise take the opportunity for a quick meal are frightened away, leaving the turtles in peace to continue a process that has been going on for hundreds of thousands of years. Turtle eggs are a delicacy for humans as well as animals, but the Costa Ricans, as natural conservationists, allow for egg-gathering only at certain times, and in regulated numbers, in order to ensure that enough baby turtles make it to the ocean when they hatch from their buried nests in the sand about a month and a half later.

It would not be an understatement to say that the arribada of the sea turtles is made possible through a cooperative effort of the sun, moon, stars, winds, oceans, earth, animals, and people. A shaman's mind recognizes that the turtles are at the center of the universe because the entire universe conspired to aid in their creation, and all shamans know that they themselves are no different than the turtles because they too are at the center of their universe.

And so are you, at the center of yours.

Indigenous people revere Nature. The reason anyone reveres anything is because they are inspired by it, they want to align with it and emulate it, and it has something to teach them. Nature's immeasurable interconnectivity and holism show us who we are. In Nature, there is no separation. Everything is connected, and if it is a cooperative and connected universe, then that means that we are each an inextricable part of that interdependence. This leads us to the second principle of Huna: *There are no limits*–no real boundaries between you and your body, between you and other people, between you and the universe, and between you and God.

We are all part of one giant organism, which means that your well-being has a substantive effect on the wellbeing of everything else. The microcosm of each of us *is* an exact template of the macrocosm of the whole. Separation, from a Huna perspective, is only an illusion. Because we are each an individual representation of the entire cosmos, we must take one hundred percent responsibility for our indivisibility with everything by recognizing that how we take care of ourselves has a direct and substantive effect on how we take care of each other. I once heard Serge Kahili King say, "If you want to heal someone, think of them and YOU feel good." We heal others by healing ourselves.

This vast interconnectivity has been validated by science. Quantum physics speaks of a "zero point" in each atom; if we could somehow enter into this point, it would lead us to *the same point in every other atom everywhere*. This idea is illustrated in a startling 1998 study undertaken by the late Dr. Sorin Sonea of the University of Montreal, who discovered what he called "the Global Organism"—new bacterial resistance to certain medications in humans that could be tracked on a worldwide scale, often within days of the initial discovery of the resistance.

If this interconnective wonder hasn't addled your brain, consider an animal-behavioral study conducted in the 1950s, called "the Hundred Monkey Effect," which proved that just as scientists on a Japanese island taught apes to wash sweet potatoes in the sea before eating them, the apes on another island simultaneously began doing the same thing without any instruction.

We exchange air, energy, and consciousness with everything on the planet and infinitely beyond, and the central axis point of this vast matrix of interconnectivity lies within each of us. Before ceremonial work, shamans traditionally invoke the six directions—East, South, West, North, Sky, and Earth—in order to center themselves into a non-dualistic framework that is a fundamental shamanic conception of reality and self: All things are indivisible from all other things, and everything that exists is available to us. The six directions are not just geographical; they each hold many beings and energies.

This limitlessness goes far beyond implied physical and energetic connection; it is also the boundlessness within our own minds that connects us to our hopes, aspirations, and dreams, and any and all means of achieving them. There is a well-known Hawaiian saying, *A'ohe pu'u ki'eki'e ke ho'a'o 'ia e pi'i,* which means, "No hill is so tall that it cannot be climbed."

Because the world is what you think it is, your perceived limitations become your world, but this second principle teaches us that *absolutely anything is possible if you can figure out how to do it.* If that seems far fetched, allow me to introduce you to the Siberian shamans who visit the Amazonian rainforest by transforming themselves into blue orbs, the Tibetan monks who can bilocate from the bottom of a mountain to the top within minutes, and the spiritualists who talk to the dead with evidentiary precision. And how about the inventions and creations of Albert Einstein, Giacomo Puccini, Marie Curie, George Washington Carver, Jane Austen, Bill Gates, the Wright Brothers, and every innovator and world-record breaker who's ever lived?

In his book *The Bowl of Light,* Hank Wesselman writes about the grandmother of a famous Kahuna who once said that there is a pervasive belief in Polynesia that there is no such thing as "I don't know"—everything exists, so everything can be known.

Separation then, is only an illusion, although it can sometimes be an extremely useful one. We separate things in order to organize, measure, or appropriately disconnect; if we didn't in some way "divide" our limitless reality, we would have no experience at all. We all need to be on time for our flight, adhere to certain laws in order to function properly in society, follow the recipe for baking delicious chocolate chip cookies, and avoid television news shows when we want to minimize stress. In many instances, separation is necessary; in Huna, we utilize it when it serves us, but we don't think of it as reality.

The shaman's mind swims in an ocean of universal connection where everything is available, anything is possible, and connection is everywhere. It's just a matter of finding it, and saying *yes.*

Kala Practice — Visioning Exercise

Because there are no limits, there is already a connection to anything that we yearn for or desire, and we bridge this connection by expanding our consciousness toward whatever it is that we want.

Take some time with the following exercise. Allow yourself to yearn for and connect with what you most desire. With Ike, we began to address our core beliefs; with Kala, we will release what divides us from the universe.

In a journal, write down at least seventy-five things you want. Don't worry about how you will get or achieve these things, and definitely don't judge any that come to mind. Whatever it is that you want, simply write them all down as if they are wishes for a genie in a bottle.

Seventy-five things may seem a lot of things, but this is on purpose, because when you include not just the obvious desires (health, finances, career, relationship, home) but also the more frivolous ones (a trip to Tulum or Venice, a Gucci watch, a new back porch, starting a book club), you'll begin to see where you have set limitations on what is possible for you, and you will even gain insight into who you are.

Be as specific as you can with everything that you list, and let go of the notion that this exercise is egotistical or selfish. Remember that one of the goals of the shaman's mind is to be so satiated that we give back to the world from surplus and abundance—so go ahead and want things with abandon!

After your list is complete, find images of all the things you want, and post those images on the desktop of your computer, or decorate your space with them. The easiest way to do this is to collect pictures online and drag them to your computer desktop or to create a document with them. Or you might find images in magazines and cut them out, which is also a great way to collect them.

You will begin to notice that certain themes emerge, such as travel, health, career, and you can group and arrange your images in any way that you like. The point here is that every time you open or turn on your computer, or look around your space, you'll make a connection to your heart's truest desires.

Begin to notice any synchronicities, signs, or events that reflect the things on yodur list. This could be a conversation you overhear, an advertisement that you see on television or in a magazine, a direct connection with something from your list, or something similar to one of your items that somehow makes itself known to you.

Naming what you want is to uncover your true identity. In doing this exercise, you may be surprised by how many things so fundamental to you have been either hidden away or remain unclaimed, even as potential desires. To name what it is that we yearn for is the first step in breaking through limitation, because, as the second Huna principle states, there is a connection to everything, if we can somehow find it.

With continued focus on the things you want, you may also begin to have the experience that these things will magically start to appear in your life. This is because of the third principle of Huna, *Makia* (pronounced Mah-key-ah), which states that where we place our focus and attention creates the energetic influence that manifests things into being.

CHAPTER SIX

ENERGY FLOWS WHERE ATTENTION GOES

Makia: To aim or strive for, to concentrate on, to purpose.

If you leave a forest alone to do its thing, that forest will continue an endless process of growth and creation. Now, there might be infighting among species: Animals may eat other animals, diseases might infect some of the plant life, seasons will come and go, and there may be a brush fire or drought. But, left to its own devices, the overall direction of that forest will always be moving toward growth and creation—this is the energy of Nature. That which moves the tides, spins the Earth, grows the trees, shines the sun, and beats your heart is made of this same energy, and it pervades everything that exists. The third principle of Huna is, "Energy flows where attention goes" — and with our concentration and our focus, we can harness the creative forces of the universe.

If you've received a high school diploma, planned a dinner party, lost twenty pounds, run a half-marathon, or supported a political candidate, then you know that it is through focus and attention that we accomplish anything. But according to Huna's third principle, there are energetic considerations at play as well—with our focus and attention, we elicit an energetic response from the universe that attracts to us the closest physical equivalent of whatever is the object of our focus and attention. In other words, what we dwell on with consistency elicits the creative energy that manifests material reality.

The implications of this principle are staggering, because it implies that we exist in a symbiotic universe that will gladly lend us some of its creative spark in response to our focused intent, and the stronger and more consistent our focus, the stronger the creative spark. And it's not just our conscious awareness; what we dwell on unconsciously—our habituated thoughts and beliefs—will have the same effect. We attract the same patterns of experience over and over again, based on where we direct our attention. So, just as changing our beliefs changes our world, shifting what we focus on shifts what we are able to create.

The third principle of Huna reminds us to take one hundred percent responsibility for ourselves, because if we are not paying attention to what we are actually paying attention to, then we are unaware of the energetic blueprints that are being created by our focus and our attention and are in a continuous process of becoming matter. Energy is neutral, neither good nor bad, and it will move toward whatever positive or negative polarity we feed with our attention. Dwell on fear and you will attract more of that which scares you; focus on love and you will beget more love; consistently affirm powerlessness and you will be mired in it; sustain your attention on writing a book on Huna and you'll find a myriad of ways and means to do just that.

Because energy flows where attention goes, energy can be transmitted non-locally to people, foreign lands, the past, the future, and our own dreams and aspirations just by focusing on them. This is, of course, the essence of prayer and of sending healing over a distance, and as discussed previously, it is a fundamental component in the alchemy of conscious manifestation, or magic. If you are unsure how to pray, do distance healing, or create magic, don't worry; your focused intent alone is enough to initiate all of them successfully—the energy will do the rest because *the energy already knows what to do.* The shaman's mind sets up the conditions for manifestation through his or her willful focus; the actual doing of it is up to the energies, while the shaman's job is just to create the focus.

A few years ago, I wanted to attract more minorities into my private practice, and I was particularly interested in working with the LGBTQ population. I could have done a social media campaign, or advertised in specifically targeted areas, but knowing that energy flows where attention goes, I decided to try a simple magical spell instead. I went to a local metaphysical store, and bought a rainbow-colored, seven-day candle, which to me represented "diversity." I also bought some powdered incense which, believe it or not, was called "Oscar Wilde"—you can find anything in New York City!

The next day, when I was in my office, I burned the incense (which, more than anything, helped me focus my mind on the task at hand, but was also related thematically) while holding the candle in my hands and concentrating on the new clients that I wanted to attract. As I allowed myself to be filled with feelings of satisfaction and joy as I visualized receiving new clients, I infused the candle with my intention and asked the universe to bring them to me. I stayed in this focused, meditative state for around thirty minutes, affirming that once I lit the candle it would send my intention out to the universe for the next seven days. I also resolved that every time I looked at the burning candle, I would be reminded to reaffirm my intention and focus on it again. It didn't take but three days before my email inbox had numerous requests from new clients requesting appointments, with a particularly noticeable influx of LGBTQ people.

I haven't the foggiest idea why this spell worked, and it isn't important that I should have, because it actually makes no logical sense whatsoever. But, based on what you have learned so far from the Huna principles, you can understand that the first one, "The world is what you think it is," required me to at least believe in spell work because, otherwise, I never would have bothered trying. The second principle, "There are no limits," confirmed that there was already a connection between me and those clients that I had yet to meet; I just had to figure out how to reach them. And the third principle, "Energy flows where attention goes," instructed me to use my focused attention to bring about the energy needed to attract the new clients.

Now, you may be wondering why it is that if manifestation using only our mind can be so easy, it sometimes does not happen. Why can't we just focus on winning the lottery and all become millionaires? And how do we know if we are focusing on the right things in the first place? To answer these questions, we need to go back to the forest.

Remember that the forest is in an endless process of growth and creation, showing us the energy of Nature, which underlies everything. If what we want to create is in alignment with *our* growth and creation, then there is a congruency with the very energy needed to create it. Creative energy is going to flow with our attention regardless of whether what we are focusing on is actually in our best interest or not. But when we are pursuing that which leads us toward our highest good and the promptings of our soul, we are in alignment with the energy of Nature itself, and the result often feels like a flowing cooperation.

If we allow ourselves to *feel without commentary*, our bodies and our emotions will always guide us in the right direction. Our *Naʻau*—our gut, or second brain—which is located a few inches below our navel, is the source of our feelings and our instincts, and if we take notice of what it is telling us, it will give us directional feedback that we can always rely on. In the past, when you took an action that was personally enriching and related to your wellbeing, you no doubt had the experience of feeling the satisfying and pleasurable emotions that accompanied it. Likewise, when you did something that was antithetical to your best interest, you probably felt unpleasant or agitating emotions emerge. In other words, the Na'au is the biological wiring that helps us to *feel* what should receive our focus and attention.

The problem is that we are often conditioned to ignore the wisdom of our emotions. How many times have you been told—or told yourself—that you "should," or "shouldn't" feel the way that you actually do? Or denied your true feelings or intentions because of the fear of financial survival if you were to act on them? Pretended you liked something that you didn't in order to go with along with your family or another group? Suffered through doing something that you knew you didn't want to do in the first place? When we stop listening to our inner directives, we can lose ourselves.

The forest, on the other hand, doesn't have the slightest doubt or conflict about who it is, or what it wants. But when doubt or conflict are present within us, then some of our focus and attention will move toward that doubt or conflict, away from that which we wish to create, and the energy that is produced will lack potency because it will mirror that conflict. Focusing on what you want and ignoring the doubt or conflict completely, is what might be called "courage" or "purpose," and in the face of either, miracles happen. The forest always reaches toward the sun, opens to the rain, extends itself downward into the soil, and grasps toward life however it can; it never turns on itself or denies itself what it yearns for or what is good for it—and if we want to be like the forest, as any shaman would, then neither should we.

What is the ultimate right direction for you? Only you and your Na'au can know for sure. That said, consider that, from a Huna perspective, nothing is "meant to be." Because the future isn't fixed, there isn't necessarily a "right direction" for anyone. Whatever happens to us is the consequence of our focus, attention, thoughts, and beliefs. But because everything is alive, aware, conscious, and responsive, there are innumerable other factors that may have nothing to do with us directly, but will nonetheless impact us. So we do not have control over anything, but we do have the ability to influence with our focused intent; more than anything, Huna's third principle, Makia, is about the *energetic influence* we each possess that is based on where we lay our focus and attention.

In the example of my candle spell, I could assume that because it was effective, my intention to attract certain clients was at least sufficiently in alignment with the creative energies of the universe for it to come to fruition. Had the spell not worked, I could have tried another process, examined my intentions around why I wanted to attract that kind of client, assumed that the timing was off, seen it as an indication that perhaps I needed to work less and not take on more clients, or used it as an opportunity to examine internal doubts I may have had about any number of factors. Energy is intelligent, so if you have given something your focused attention and removed any doubt and conflict, then you can allow yourself to trust what you get, learn from it, and assume that the outcome is actually the best one for you at that time.

Lastly, I want to explore one more facet of Makia, one that I hope ignites your imagination and playfulness. I have referred to the energy that flows with our attention and focus as being akin to the creative energy of Nature. However, the shaman thinks of Nature not only as what we experience when we go outdoors, but also as including the entirety of the spiritual realms. To the shaman, all guides, angels, ascended masters, devas, elementals, gnomes, fairies, and dwarfs are as real as the rainforests. So your own personal aesthetic and gnosis may guide you to relate to energy as the spiritual influence of Jesus, the Wiccan goddess Hecate, the volcano goddess Pele, the Archangel Michael, the pagan god Pan, the feathered-serpent god of the Aztecs Quetzelcoatl, the Buddha, the Ancestors, Santería's ocean mother goddess Yemaya, or beings of the Fairy realms.

It can be supportive and healing to think of wise and loving beings responding to our thoughts and our attention, and although it is not necessary that you do so, if it helps or pleases you to personify energy in this way, then by all means do. Developing relationships with spirit guides or spirit beings requires nothing more than an imaginative curiosity about them, and a willingness to engage them in relationship. Remember that the world is what you think it is, you are at the center of the universe, and what you focus on creates your experience. Ask these benevolent beings to work with you, and because they are already a part of you, created by your focus and attention, they will.

Makia Practices

"Energy following thought" is one of the most important concepts in Huna, so I have included a few Makia practices that you can work with experientially. Remember that shamans are expert facilitators; they don't *do* the magic or create the energy, they bring about the circumstances that allows them to happen of their own accord. Energy is in response to the mind's machinations, not the other way around. A good adage for the following exercises is: "Intend, and then get out of the way." In other words, you are only responsible for focusing your attention on the tasks at hand, and the energy of the universe will do what it will. Ride it wherever it takes you.

Makia Practice — Pikopiko Breathing

Pikopiko is a simple breathing technique from the Kahili tradition that creates energetic effects by placing our awareness on certain parts of the body. In Hawaiian, *piko* means "navel," "umbilical cord," and also "genitals." In old Hawaii, some islanders would facetiously greet each other by saying, "*Pehea kou piko*," or "How's your piko?" Because the early Christian missionaries traveling to the Hawaiian Islands were not aware of the kaona or hidden meanings of many Hawaiian words, the native islanders are said to have relished the bawdy double meaning of this phrase as they greeted their new neighbors with it. Today, because the navel is considered a spiritual point on the body, it has a deeper meaning among Hawaiians, which is something like, "How is your inner light?"

Like so many Hawaiian words, there are opposite meanings contained in piko as well, such as "summit at the top of a mountain" and "crown of the head." The main pikos that we will use in *pikopiko* breathing are the navel and the crown of the head, but we will also include other pikos, or centers of focus, that are outside the body.

The instructions for the practice are quite simple. Read them over slowly, or record them with your own voice so that you can follow along with the words. Remember that you are not trying to move or create energy as you do pikopiko breathing, or to make anything specific happen at all; *you are simply breathing while simultaneously placing your full awareness on each point mentioned.*

Repeat the following sequence as much as you like; as you do, you will notice currents of energy moving through and around you. This breathing practice can have many different effects, so allow your experience of it to be uniquely your own.

Inhale with your attention at your crown of your head, exhale with your attention at your navel. Inhale with your attention at your navel, exhale with your attention at your crown of your head. (Repeat at least five times.)

Inhale with your attention a few feet above you, exhale with your attention at your navel. Inhale with your attention at your navel, exhale with your attention a few feet below you. Inhale with your attention a few feet below you, exhale with your attention at your navel. Inhale with your attention at your navel, exhale with your attention a few feet above you. (Repeat at least five times.)

Inhale with your attention at the sun and stars, exhale with your attention at your navel. Inhale with your attention on the center of the earth, exhale with your attention at your navel. (Repeat at least five times.)

Inhale and imagine all the energy around you, exhale with all that energy at your navel. Inhale with all that energy at your navel, exhale to all the energy around you. (Repeat at least five times.)

You may wish to record your experience of this practice in a journal.

Makia Practice — Kahi

Kahi, which is derivative of the traditional Lomi-Lomi massage of Hawaii, is translated as "to press or stroke, as in a massage" or "pressure with the open palm of the hand." It is a simple laying-on-of-hands practice, and it too comes from the Kahili family tradition. Kahi synchronizes our focus and attention with our hands to produce healing energy.

Because this is such a simple practice, it is probably more important to address some common misconceptions about hands-on healing before I give you the instructions. When students first learn to utilize touch for healing, they often assume that they are to use their own personal energy to "send into" another or think they are to "take away" (or possibly "take on") the "bad" energy. To a certain extent, these methods can be effective, but they are unhealthy and unnecessary. As we have discussed, our focus and attention is the only invitation that energy needs to start engaging with us. The shaman facilitates healing with his intent, and the energies do the rest. Kahi asks us to lay our hands on the body, so we will focus our attention on them, and *that's all that we have to do.* Here's how to practice Kahi:

Intuit one area of your or another person's body that you think might need some healing, such as the forehead, heart, throat, navel, or hip, and place one hand there, with your palm open and facing down. Then choose another point on the body that will serve as a "power spot," somewhere that you sense is healthy and strong, and place your other, open-palmed hand there. As you may have experienced with pikopiko breathing, energy moves between two points of attention, and in kahi, these two points are those where we place our hands.

These two areas might correspond to energy centers or the chakras, but they can also be anywhere on the body. Let your intuition guide you. It is not necessary that one point be necessarily weaker; you might intend to further strengthen an area on the body that you sense is already healthy and strong.

After you have placed your hands on both points, allow them to be still while you put your attention and focus on each point at the same time. If focusing on both points simultaneously is challenging for you, you can simply move your attention and your focus back and forth quickly between the open palms of each of your hands.

If you are working with another person, a good variation is to place both of your hands on two points on their body. Then inhale with your attention on your own navel, and exhale with your attention on both of your hands and where they are touching your partner's body. Repeat this process for at least three slow breaths. In this partnered variation, your navel (though you might experiment with using your heart or another part of your body as well) will serve as the power spot, and both of the points where your hands are resting on your partner's body will receive your focus for healing.

As you practice Kahi, you will begin to notice energy moving between each point of attention where you have placed your hands.

Just for fun, experiment with imagining a rainbow, a waterfall, or a light with the color of your choosing flowing between your two hands.

You may wish to record your experience of this practice in a journal; or, if you worked with a partner, you can share your experience of it with each other.

Candle Magic

Because this is a book on Huna, I initially hesitated to include a section on candle magic, which comes from the Western occult traditions. But while working with candles is not a Hawaiian practice *per se*, I have found it to be an extremely helpful way to work experientially with the Huna principles that you have learned thus far.

Fire, which has been used in magic and ritual since Paleolithic times, is a symbol of transmutation, the alchemical process of changing form from one thing to another. Shamans have traditionally regarded fire as an intelligent elemental spirit, an ancestral being that holds the secrets of the origins of life and the mysteries of death and rebirth. Fire symbolizes action, passion, and sensual creation; for our purposes, you might think of it as a conscious beacon for Makia, or for our focus and attention.

The candle itself symbolizes that which we wish to create by doing this spell. The size, type (soy, beeswax etc.), and color are really up to you. In general, a seven-day candle can be very helpful, because it lends extra time to the process, but any kind of candle will do. You might like to use one that can burn safely in glass while you are away from your space. The spell will work whether or not the candle burns continuously, and in fact, every time you relight it will provide another opportunity to focus on your intent. But, whichever you chose, be sure to consider safety above all else.

There is a lot of material available on the magical correspondences of different colors, but what truly matters is what the color of the candle symbolizes for you. Green may represent a lucrative new job, blue might symbolize the ocean for a South Pacific vacation you want to manifest, white could be for forgiveness or healing, and a red candle may represent the way you are trying to put a stop to something. If you are unsure which color to use, orange is representative of the third principle in the Kahili tradition, and you are welcome to use that if it suits you.

There is no right way to do this spell, but here are some general guidelines. It is important to be very clear about what you want to manifest: Be sure that you are willing to receive it, and lay all of your doubts aside. While this spell will get some energy moving toward your goal, the best time to do magical work is after you have done everything in your power in a real-world way to make something happen, so make sure you have been taking your own actions for what you want to create as well.

It is your focused attention that fuels any magic, so you'll want to carve out time when you can give it your all. Imbuing your physical space with sacredness and purposeful intent will help to increase your focus. If you recall, I used specific incense to help me to do this, but adding any sensual elements—sounds, tastes, scents, etc.—will do the same. You also might try taking a conscious and mindful ritual bath to get into the right "head space" for the task at hand. The ancient Hawaiians called this ceremonial bath for spiritual purification *kapu kai*.

Lastly, remember to connect emotionally with your intention: Manifest feelings of excitement and satisfaction as you imagine what you want and the possibility of receiving it. Emotional investment not only strengthens your focus, but also helps to override doubt. Remember that this is a process between you and the energies of the universe, so really advocate for yourself, and invest your heart and soul into the process.

1. *Choose what you would like to create, and be very clear on the specific outcome that you want.*

2. *Prepare your space and yourself (music, scents, ritual bath, meditation).*

3. *Hold your candle in your hands and build up your energy with some pikopiko breathing.*

4. *As you hold the candle, fill your mind with thoughts, images, feelings, and emotions about the subject of your spell. Imagine yourself receiving what you want, and petition the energies (or "guides," if you like) directly and sincerely to bring it to you.*

5. *Create a strong intention that the candle will "hold" that which you wish to create, and affirm that in each instant that it burns, its flame is inviting the energies of creation.*

6. *Light your candle. As it burns, strongly affirm that the magic has begun and is now in the process of happening.*

7. *Throughout the entire time that your candle is burning, every time you think of it, or look at your candle, reaffirm and revisualize your intention.*

8. *Over the coming days and weeks, keep your eyes open. Remember that we use Makia to influence, but there are innumerable other factors at play. Trust what you get, learn from it, and assume that all results are for the best.*

These Makia practices are meant to get you started working with energy, but remember that you create energetic influence every time you think a thought. The shaman's mind never forgets the practical magic that is made possible simply by turning on the light of our attention and our focus. It is through our conscious awareness that endless opportunities become available to us in every moment, and the fourth Huna principle, *Manawa* (pronounced Muh-nah-wah), teaches us that there is no moment that contains more power than the one that you are experiencing right now.

CHAPTER SEVEN

NOW IS THE MOMENT OF POWER

Manawa: A period of time, turn, date, season, or chronology.

There was once a pious and reverent man who lived in a modest home in a small town by the sea. He had unquestionable faith in God, and he believed that no matter what, God would always take care of him and protect him. He prayed regularly, attended church weekly, and was a pillar of his community.

One day, the civic authorities alerted everyone in the town that a tsunami had been detected far out at sea and was on its way. For fear of immanent destruction and danger, everyone was told to evacuate immediately.

Public buses rushed around the community, picking up people to drive them to higher ground and safety. This pious man was the only one in the entire town who did not leave on one of the buses. He stayed in his house, affirming to himself, "I have the upmost faith in God's love and protection, and I trust that He will always have mercy on me."

The tsunami hit with even greater force than expected, and the town flooded completely. The water level rose even higher than the height of most men. As the surge continued to rise, the pious man climbed out through a window in his home and sat on his rooftop. In no time, a speed boat approached and a crewman yelled to him to jump into the boat so that he could be rescued. The pious man again professed his faith in his Creator, and refused the invitation.

As the water began to rise above his rooftop, the pious man climbed up to the top of the chimney. The water continued to rise. A helicopter appeared, hovering above the pious man's house. A rope ladder was thrown down to him and the helicopter pilot shouted through a megaphone at the man, telling him to grab on tight. The man yelled back that he had no need. "God is good and merciful," he shouted. "I trust in His protection totally!" The helicopter flew away, and the water continued to rise until it finally washed the man off the chimney. Within a few minutes, he was lost in the floodwater, and quickly drowned.

He found himself inside the pearly gates of Heaven, as angels hovered and celestial harp music played. God the Almighty appeared and looked down on him with kind and smiling eyes. Kneeling before God, the pious man said, "Heavenly Father, I don't understand. I always trusted in you totally. What happened? Why did you forsake me?" God shrugged his shoulders, rolled his eyes and said, "Buddy, I don't know what to tell you. I sent you a bus, a boat, and a helicopter!"

This ham-handed segue brings us to the fourth principle of Huna, which states that every instant is a chance to save ourselves, a new opportunity for change, for choice, and for rewriting our story. It is in the present moment that true power exists because it is only there that we are able to do anything. The past is gone—dead and buried. The future is not yet born: *Now is the moment of power.*

Since the Chinese invasion of Tibet in 1950, and the mass exportation to the West that followed soon afterward of Buddhistic and Yogic wisdom from India and beyond, Eastern spiritual systems have exploded into Western culture. Meditation and mindfulness are now considered so mainstream and scientifically legitimate that they have transcended the monastery and the ashram and have entered into hospitals, universities, and the media. The word "now" is contained within the titles of some of today's most cherished spiritual books. It seems that everyone is talking about the importance of being fully present in every moment.

Because there is so much information already available on mindfulness and meditation, I won't spend much time extolling the virtues of either. In fact, I can sum up the importance and healing potential of both with a simple saying from my first meditation teacher, who often said, "You have to be present to win." So, instead of focusing on the agitated "monkey mind" that is often referenced in Buddhist practice, I want to examine how we *create* in the here-and-now, for, in Huna, the power of the present moment is the action that we take within it. A mystic might want to sit peacefully in a meditative state of present-time awareness, but a shaman wants to *do* something with it.

Now is the moment of power. Since *now* is the only moment that *contains* power, now is the only place where we can access it. The past has no impact on us other than what we decide it has, because the past endures solely in memory, and a memory is nothing more than a story (and a selectively remembered one at that) that we can reinterpret, recreate, or rewrite however we like. The future is nothing more than embryonic potential, the fruition of which is entirely dependent on the actions and choices that we take *in the now*. In fact, Huna philosophy says that because our universe is limitless, all time exists simultaneously in the present moment. If that is true, then we are connected to the power that exists within each present moment to change and influence the past or the future in any way we consciously choose.

Who you are right now is not a representation of who you have been in the past, nor of who you might be in the future; it is no more nor less than who you think you are in this moment. I can already hear some of you grumbling, "But such and such happened to me, of course it still affects me now!" While that might be true for you, it doesn't have to be. You may have to do some forgiveness work for yourself or others, recalibrate your identity a bit, change some rules or bottom lines that you have created for yourself or those around you, and pull your frame of reference back far enough to see that your past suffering need not be in vain if you now decide to use it as an opportunity for growth. The only place where you can make these changes is in the present moment, and if you decide that this is what *now* is for you, then that is what *now* becomes. In every moment, we can choose to start over.

Huna's third principle tells us that to focus on anything is to stir the winds of creation, while the fourth reminds us that we can only do so right now. Even the genetic predispositions in our DNA or the Karmic lessons of the soul that we are to learn in this lifetime will only come to fruition insofar as how they similarly align with our present-moment thoughts, beliefs, and intentions. Nothing is predetermined, because all of our inherent propensities are under the influence of what we are presently creating with our minds. Similarly, the habits that we have constructed by repeatedly strengthening them through our past actions can be released whenever we like, because in any moment we can begin the habit of a new habit. *Now* is where we create our lives, and when it is free of past regrets and future fears, it is an immensely friendly place of fertile ground.

In working with my own clients I've noticed that it is not that people are unaware of the present moment or absent-minded about it; rather, they are fully engaged with it while co-creating an absolute mess. They usually do this in one of three ways: first, by pretending that what's happening isn't really happening and not feeling their feelings; second, by scaring the bejesus out of themselves with their thoughts; and third, by using their thoughts to self-annihilate. When we take one hundred percent responsibility for our relationship with the present moment, we settle into the one true place where power resides. So let's examine the three ways in which we sometimes use the power of the present moment to our own detriment.

There is an old adage that warns us, "Nothing good ever happens after midnight." While that might be true, an even better one is: "Nothing good ever happens from not being in your body." Our bodies are where our emotions and our feelings reside, and if we are disconnected from them, then we are separated from our deepest truth. When we pretend that what is really happening inside us isn't happening, or we deny that it is, we perpetuate the destructive habit of pulling away from our bodies, and ignoring our feelings and emotions. This is a kind of self-violence in which we turn against the very parts of ourselves with which we should have the most intimate rapport.

The shaman aspires to emulate Nature, even though there are plenty of things in Nature that we might not like: cockroaches, great white sharks, tornados, and tarantulas, for example. While these beings are probably not among our favorites, we would never think that they should not exist. Yet that is exactly how we relate to ourselves when we don't allow our feelings and our emotions to be as they truly are. When we judge, negate, or deny our feelings and emotions, we lock ourselves out of our own hearts, and we rob ourselves of the vital information that they contain.

Our feelings and emotions are the way that Nature expresses itself through each of us, and just like all things in Nature, our feelings and emotions happen spontaneously of their own accord. You don't "decide" to experience fear, anger, joy, or even a sexual response—they simply happen as they do, just as Nature does. Therefore, ignoring or judging our feelings is akin to standing by a seashore and yelling at the waves to stop crashing, or looking at a tree while insisting that it should somehow look differently than it does, or standing in the rain and wondering why you're wet, or trying to teach a tiger to become a vegetarian.

Now is the moment of power, because *now* is where we can feel the wisdom of our emotions, and your recognition and acceptance of them—even *your own* cockroaches, great white sharks, tornados, and tarantulas, which may manifest as your anger, fear, jealousy, or lust— creates the compassionate acknowledgement that becomes the free- dom to do something skillfully about them. Whatever occurs does so for a reason, and by allowing it to be just as it is, we can start to figure out what the reason is.

The second type of *now* that we must seek to avoid is the one in which we use our thoughts to terrify ourselves. Fear plays an integral part in self-preservation, but more often than not, it leads to paralysis. Fear is a confusing emotion because it feels so unpleasant, and yet its presence often indicates healthy development. If we aren't coming up against a modicum of fear from time to time, we probably aren't growing. In fact, when a client tells me of being scared of doing something that would lead to growth, the subtext is often: "That means I don't have to do X, Y, or Z, right?" Fear can be used as an excuse to exempt us from responsibility.

Life is an endless process of becoming ourselves more fully, and as we develop, heal, and grow, we can find ourselves caught in the gap between an old sense of self that no longer serves us and a new sense of self that we have not yet fully realized. I call this liminal space "the Danger Zone"—an in-between and unfamiliar place where we know that we are not who we once were, but we have yet to become who we are growing into being.

When we are in the Danger Zone, fear often predominates. We can't quite find the ground beneath our feet, and we often retreat backwards to familiar yet outdated ways of being. The Danger Zone can be intimidating, scary, and a real crisis of identity; navigating it requires faith, along with the steadfast affirmation that everything is part of a larger process. We can alleviate the fear and unease that inevitably present themselves on our journey toward wholeness by remembering that *the in-between place is still a place.*

The language we use in the present moment is also very significant when it comes to minimizing fear. There is a huge difference between someone telling me that they are "lost" or "a mess" and hearing someone say, *"Jonathan, I am really going through it."* I'll take the latter any day of the week and twice on Sunday, because the former examples imply entrenched and fixed states, while the latter implies movement. There is an emotional neutrality in going through it, while the states of being lost or a mess are fearfully charged with a sense of permanence. We must always build a crack of light into the present moment, a portal through which choice and solutions are always accessible. The second Huna principle reminds us that there are endless possibilities, but we scare ourselves when we use emotionally-charged language that indicates fixed and forever states. Creating a *now* that is full of fear is never an appropriate way for us to stay vigilant; it doesn't keep us in line, or help to avert disaster. Energy flows where attention goes, and focusing on fear just perpetuates more of it.

If you recall, the beautiful Hawaiian phrase *"E aloha ia 'oe iho me like aloha 'oe ia Ke Akua Nui"* reminds us to "Love yourself as you love God." The converse of this wise guidance occurs when we self-annihilate with our thoughts, which is the third way that we turn against ourselves in the present moment. "Annihilation" is a very dramatic word, and I choose it intentionally because it indicates how damaging it is to engage in it. But before addressing what to do about self-annihilation, I want to unpack why we engage in it in the first place.

There is a particular phenomenon that pervades the Western psyche, in which an imprinted pattern of "wrongness" is linked to our fundamental sense of self. It's a sinking feeling that tells us that no matter what, we are absolutely never to think of ourselves as fundamentally okay. Whether we are focused on our physical appearance, our body, how much money we make, the level of success we think we have achieved, our intelligence, our social standing, or our sexuality, somehow we have learned to merge our identity with a deep sense of wrongness.

We can spend our lives trying to escape the dread of finding out that some awful truth about us may have validity. Often, we try to keep this fear at bay by accomplishing things, creating attractive (and sometimes false) appearances, being generally "good people," isolating ourselves from others and remaining on the sidelines or armoring our hearts for protection. But just underneath the surface, like a crocodile's eye peering out from beneath the watery depths, the deep doubt we hold about our fundamental sense of self waits for its opportunity to attack us.

When we are invalidated, rejected, or even when we just receive bad news, we take this as evidence of our wrongness, and berate and annihilate ourselves for it. If we don't get the job promotion, if someone doesn't text us back, if we're left at the altar, if our work is criticized, or when we see on billboards impossible standards of beauty that we can't possibly hope to achieve, we make the grave assumption that these dynamics point to something intrinsically flawed about us. Negative feedback from the outside world, or even the possibility of it, becomes the validation of the "bad thing" that we are so afraid we might be—and off we will go, berating ourselves again.

As we will examine more fully when we reach the sixth principle Mana, we are all a spark of the divine, and to see ourselves as anything other than this is to engage in an illusion. This means that nothing that happens to us is ever an indication of something fundamentally flawed about us, it's just what's happening. We must trust that our inherent goodness always remains. Self-annihilation is a waste of time and energy because it obscures the manifold prospects of the present moment, and it sends us on a wild goose chase to find, to hide, or to correct something that we think might be true, but that actually doesn't even exist.

To close this section on Manawa, I'll share an anecdote from my days as an actor. Years ago, I had the good fortune to play one of the juiciest roles in all of Shakespeare, the ne'er-do-well Mercutio in *Romeo and Juliet.* Mercutio is not a very large role; in fact, this member of the Montague family dies halfway through the play on the sword of a rival Capulet. He also doesn't have all that much to say in the play, except for one scene in Act One, when, to a drunken audience of a few of his rambunctious and concupiscent adolescent buddies, he teases Romeo about his lovelorn ways by reciting Shakespeare's famous speech about Queen Mab.

Mercutio's Queen Mab soliloquy is long, rambling, mythic, poetic, bawdy, nonsensical, hilarious, banal, and just plain odd. It does nothing to service the plot of the play, nor does it contribute to character development in any way. It goes on and on for hundreds of lines, and for the life of me, I could not begin to figure out what purpose it served. I toiled with it for weeks in rehearsal, flailing and prancing about, experimenting with funny voices, and trying to make sense of it from every conceivable angle, but nothing seemed to work.

Then, one day I had a much needed epiphany. The whole point of the Queen Mab speech, I realized, was that there was absolutely no point at all. Mercutio talked on and on simply because he could, and it pleased him to do so. The key to playing him lay in knowing that the only thing that mattered to Mercutio was *the quality of the present moment*. He had no worries, no cares, no foresight, and no intentions other than to make an absolute feast of the *now*, presenting himself squarely in the center of it, while celebrating and serving up the multifarious joys of its possibilities for himself and everyone with whom he came into contact.

While few of us can live up to Mercutio's glorious example, he exemplifies something extraordinary about a truth that is always held in the shaman's mind: *Now is the moment, the only moment of power.*

Manawa Practice — Reframing the Past in the Present

Because the present moment is the place of power, we can change or influence anything from within it. The shaman helps to shift the meaning of hardships or difficulties by altering what they represent or symbolize: This is a basic premise of shamanic healing, and reframing or adjusting our perspective on past events is a simple and effective way to do it.

As you do this exercise, consider that humans are always trying to get their needs met, no matter what. Every action that we take is an earnest attempt to do this, though we don't always know the best way, because we may lack the knowledge or life experience to make the "right" choices. Any action that we have taken in the past that has caused us guilt or shame can be viewed entirely differently when we remember that *it is impossible to have known what we previously didn't know.* While this may seem rather obvious here, it is a source of needless suffering for many of my clients.

The following exercise will help you understand the efficacy of what the present moment can do to transform your long-held negative stories. Read through it first, or record it as a guided meditation. And, after you have completed it, you also might like to record your thoughts about it in a journal.

Take a few moments to relax, and begin to make deep inward contact with yourself. Take a few conscious inhales and exhales, just to center yourself into the present moment. If you are comfortable doing so, you can close your eyes.

Now, bring to mind a few big mistakes that you have made in your life: bad habits, instances where you didn't behave well, or actions that have caused you guilt, shame, or regret—all those what-on-Earth-was-I-thinking?! moments.

As these instances come to mind, consider that with each unfortunate event, even though your actions were unskillful, you were actually trying to do something, or to meet a need.

With as much compassion for yourself as you can possibly muster, feel into different truths about your past actions. Ask yourself—What was I actually trying to do when I behaved in this way? Was I trying to

*make something better, or was I trying to make myself feel better? Was
I attempting to help myself in some way? Was I trying to understand
something about myself? Was I hoping to alleviate some internal pain
or confusion?*

*Now, totally side with and completely befriend your past behavior.
The fact is that you didn't know what you didn't know. You didn't
know the extent of the hurt that you were causing, and you didn't realize what the negative effects would be.*

*Were you acting from innocence, or possibly from ignorance? Were
you behaving from hurt, or trying to hurt less in some way?*

What were you actually trying to do?

*Consider the fourth Huna principle, "Now is the moment of power,"
as you reframe these difficult situations with kindness and compassion
for yourself. In this moment, you can choose to see even your weakest
moments differently. Decide from this moment onward to let your new
way of seeing these actions or events in the past become a new truth or
reality.*

To understand ourselves compassionately is one of the most loving
and healing things that we can do. While many of us would naturally
extend this courtesy to others, we often fall short in doing it for ourselves. The present moment offers a powerful opportunity to create a
new story by transforming longstanding resentments, mistakes, and
confusions into necessary steps on your path.

Manawa Practice — Watching Your Thoughts

*For an entire day, or even a weekend, pay meticulous attention to your
thoughts in each moment. What energy are you running through your
system with your thoughts? What are you continually telling yourself?
Do you tend to dwell on negativity or positivity? Do you avoid your feelings, or pretend that what is happening is not happening? Do you scare*

yourself with your thoughts? Do you self-annihilate or berate yourself?
Is your thinking fixed and stagnant, or spacious and allowing? Ask
yourself, "Is what I am thinking right now good for me?"

It has been estimated that we have seventy thousand thoughts a
day—sixty-nine thousand and nine hundred and ninety-nine of which
we had yesterday. What kind of NOW do you habitually create when
almost all of your thoughts come from yesterday? Start paying attention
right now.

The present moment is a miraculous and fertile place, because it is
there that we can use our loving intentions to start anew. Aloha is the
fifth principle of Huna, and it states that the depth of our love directly
correlates to the depth our happiness. The shaman's mind has one
true directive: to seek love at all costs, and follow love wherever it
may lead.

CHAPTER EIGHT

TO LOVE IS TO BE HAPPY WITH

Aloha: Love, compassion, affection, mercy, sympathy, kindness, grace, charity.

You probably know the old song, "Love Makes the World Go Round." To the shaman, this is not merely a colloquial way of saying, "Being nice matters," it's also a precise description of the underlying intention that is the causative source of everything in existence: Love literally sets the universe in motion. Why else would the forest always move in the direction of growth and creation other than its loving and joyful intention to experience more of itself?

According to the fifth Huna principle, *Aloha*, love and happiness intertwine. Aloha teaches us that the depth of our love is the extent to which whatever it is that we love brings us happiness, and to share that happiness is a powerful means for change: *To love is to be happy with.*

What I have never understood about contemporary psychology, and most clinical approaches to health and wellness, is that love is not considered to be an integral part of the practitioner's skillset. Not only is love a potent tool, but for the shaman, it is *the* tool. At the root of any illness or disease (physical or otherwise) there is always some sort of conflict, tension, separation, or depletion. Aloha is the polar opposite of those discordant energies, and its etymology indicates its deeper meanings: *Alo* means "to share an experience," *oha* means "affection" or "joy," and *ha* translates as "breath" or "life force." To Hawaiians, Aloha is a connective and cooperative experience, one in which sharing the energy of life with another is the formula for joy.

In today's world, striving for happiness is often considered naïve, simplistic, and unrealistic. We fancy ourselves to be too driven, too smart, too practical, or too world weary to buy into happiness completely. The collective threshold for our own suffering and self-compromise is extremely high because we exist in a contemporary culture that subtly terrorizes us through its endless messaging of formulaic "goals" and "rules for living," to which we are all supposed to adhere. We are either falling short of, or prospering in, the acceptable status quo, based on some version of the conventional story of grade school, high school, university, marriage, children, job, money, "success," retirement, pension, death—and, if we have been particularly good, some sort of paradise in the hereafter. It matters far less how life *feels* as long as it *looks* a certain way, and according to those standards, happiness is rather low on the list of life's priorities.

But, as Alan Watts once said, "The point of life isn't really to get anywhere in particular, it's more of a musical thing, and we're supposed to dance." The Hawaiians have a saying, *A'a i ka hula, waiho i ka maka'u i ka hale*, which means, "Dare to dance the Hula, and leave shame at home." For shamans, love and happiness are not unrealistic ideals, but *the means for evaluating every choice that they make* for themselves, and in their guidance of others. To take one hundred percent responsibility for having a loving, co-creative involvement with life, we must insist that our every step includes love's perspective.

To the shaman, love is the basis for all creation. When we choose love, we form an allegiance with the organizing and generative principle of the cosmos. In Huna, love is the only ethic, the only rule that we must always adhere to. Love becomes the litmus test that helps us decide what choices are best for us, and how we are to live. To be in a state of Aloha is to have a positive and loving attitude toward everything (including ourselves), and to be an active participant in the creation of happiness.

Love's highest qualities, which include forgiveness, charity, understanding, and acceptance, depend upon our conscious intention to create them, and they only occur through a coming together or a harmonization of energies. Aloha is not just a feeling or a state of being, it is an active behavior, a practice that conjoins everything back to oneness. To embrace the spirit of Aloha is to build a friendlier rapport with all of life, to collaborate with it in transformative ways that lead to dynamic new beginnings. As the Hawaiian proverb *He kehau hoʻomaʻemaʻe ke aloha* reminds us: "Love is like a cleansing dew."

From what I have observed in my private practice, many people have an incomplete relationship with love. This isn't a misanthropic point of view; people are quite capable of loving deeply, but they often don't engage love to the extent needed to create the lives they want. They often have internal impediments—mental habits of criticism and judgment—which then give rise to what Serge Kahili King calls "the FUDS," or the fear, unhappiness, doubt, and stress that constrict the openness, flow, and generosity that make the existence of Aloha possible. A simple Hawaiian aphorism for living well is *aloha i nā mea a pau āu e ʻike pū ai me ʻoe iho*, which means: "Love all you see, including yourself." Nothing diminishes our ability to follow this wise instruction more than when we engage in criticism and judgment.

Huna's third principle states that the more we put our focus and attention on positivity, the more positivity we will bring into being. This principle applies for negativity as well, of course. When we criticize or judge, we are actually increasing and strengthening whatever it is that we are criticizing or judging. If you consider the synonyms for the words *criticism* and *judgment*, such as "condemnation," "fault-find-ing," and "censure," you can see that they themselves act as a kind of punishment, emphasizing negative qualities which, from a Huna per-spective, will only cause those very qualities to proliferate. Criticism and judgment are divisive, and anything that divides and separates diminishes love. An old Hawaiian saying about teamwork, which could equally be applied to love, reads, *Pūpūkahi i holomua*: "We must unite to move forward."

Further—and you may have to sit with this one for a moment—because the world is what you think it is, which means that the outside world is a reflection of that which exists inside of you, whenever we criticize or judge, we are expressing externally the exact same nega-tivity that already resides in us. From a Huna perspective, if you find yourself with something to criticize, that something was created by your own thoughts: *Have you ever noticed that whenever there is a problem, or you become aware of a problem, you're always there?*

To practice Aloha, however, is to intend confluence and unity—to become happy *with* something—and nothing does this more than praise and affirmation. If you bring to mind a time in your life when another person gave you a compliment or well wishes that you allowed yourself to fully accept, you will recall a profound feeling of wellbeing, together with a growth or expansion of whatever quality was being complimented. Whenever you bless or praise, you are helping to cre-ate more that is praiseworthy and admirable. And, according to Huna, the positive qualities that you express outwardly are a reflection of the same positive qualities that are already within you. *Have you ever noticed that whenever something wonderful happens, or you become aware of something wonderful happening, you're always there too?*

I remember being on a jungle trek through the rainforests of Belize when I came across the largest and most powerful waterfall that I had ever seen. It gushed with intensity and furor, and created winds and mists so strong that, despite my being more than thirty feet away from it, I was unable to look directly at it. I had to cover my eyes, and could only take short, squinting looks. As I felt its massive force and listened to its thunderous sounds, I felt exhilaration and astonishment, as if I were in the presence of a magnificent and holy being. I jubilantly shouted words of praise, awe, and excitement to the others who were on that same trek with me.

Then something amazing happened. Something within me began to "match" the waterfall's power. An intense force began to surge up from inside me—my chest swelled outwardly; my breath deepened; I felt my legs root deeper into the riverbed; I threw my arms open widely as if I were trying to make myself larger; and my emotions expanded into feelings of power, courage, and joy. I already had the same qualities within myself that the waterfall possessed. It was reflecting back a power inside of me that was already there; otherwise, how could I have experienced it?

In Huna, the act of blessing is considered an art in and of itself. It is a key Kapua (magical) talent because when we bless ourselves or others, we are engaging in the alchemy of bringing to ourselves the very things that we bless. The shaman's mind always seeks out that which can be loved, admired, praised, and appreciated, because whatever receives this focus and attention will grow, endure, and further create more of the same. In other words, Aloha is itself the creative force for more Aloha!

Now, there is a slight danger in writing about the power of love, because love is often bandied about as "that which heals all ills." That view can result in the misleading notion that if we just love enough, we don't have to worry about anything else. This common misunderstanding can lead to the creation of what I call the Too Good Person (TGP). The TGP focuses primarily on others, and operates under the belief that they are supposed to be perpetually nice, accepting, and tolerant of everything around them, no matter what. They often work really hard to understand and empathize with another's mistreatment, bypass or pathologize their own emotions, dissociate from their own needs, engage in one-sided or non-reciprocal relationships, and lack healthy boundaries. They might even create "gratitude lists," despite having very little for which to be truly grateful.

Practicing Aloha doesn't mean that you will never have a negative emotion again. Sometimes the single most loving thing we can do is to honor our anger, resentment, sadness, or jealousy, because each emotion contains vital information that helps us to recognize when we are in a compromised situation, or when there is something else that needs our attention.

The Hawaiians have a term, '*Ano'ai*, which can be translated as a greeting or a salutation to something which is "perhaps unexpected." The term's individual parts offer deeper meanings: '*ano'ano* means "seed," and '*ai* is "to eat" or "to bring it within." This guides us to welcome the unexpected with warmth and friendliness. There is a seed of truth in everything that we experience, and our job is not to avoid that truth, but to swallow it whole so that we can grow from it. In this way, Aloha can be present even in perceived negative circumstances; it simply depends on whether Aloha is there, or if it isn't, and only you can make that determination.

The key to not being a TGP is embedded in the second part of Huna's fifth principle: *to be happy with*. If, for whatever reason, sharing your love with another person does not create happiness, then *that is an indication that you are somewhere you are not supposed to be, or you are engaging in a relationship or a situation that you need to reexamine.*

The shaman's mind knows that energy always seeks to balance itself, and that Nature itself is a vast, cooperative effort. This means that, from a shamanic perspective, if you are involved in relationships or in life circumstances that are not reciprocal—where the amount that you invest is in great disparity with what is being returned—then you are doing something that is energetically discordant, that is not mirrored in Nature, and that is most definitely out of alignment with Aloha.

Serge Kahili King once told me, "If Aloha is given and not given back in some form, then there is no further obligation to give it."

The purest form of love is attention. We all need to be attended to, to be seen and felt by others. We need to know that we matter, and to be held in mutuality in all of our relationships. Aloha, the fifth principle of Huna, teaches us that love nourishes and satisfies through the giving *and* the receiving of it; in fact, both must happen in order for us to be able to engage it fully. And it is in this sharing of love that we find happiness.

Aloha Practice — Blessing What You Want

One of the most profound and transformative Huna practices is blessing, which is a cornerstone practice in the Kahili tradition. The instructions are quite simple: You are to affirm, compliment, praise, admire, show gratitude to, or bless anything that comes into your awareness that is exactly what you want, or even just symbolic of it.

Remember, as you do this practice, it is important to be as genuine as possible, so manifest positive emotions about whatever you're blessing. Even if what you are praising or complimenting is only symbolic of what you want (for example, blessing someone else's loving relationship), as long as you are blessing in earnest, then you are engaging in the dynamic force of Aloha.

This may be a mainly internal practice, so it is not important that you necessarily share your blessings with anyone. As you engage with the loving energies of Aloha, you will start to notice beautiful shifts and changes within yourself, and eventually in your external life as well. The more that you remember to practice blessing, the more impressive your results will be.

Here are some examples of blessing, and I encourage you to create your own as well:

✓ *If you want a better body, praise and bless those in movies, magazines, or at the gym who have bodies that you admire.*

✓ *If you want more money, bless any money that comes to you, or anything that you see in the world that money created.*

✓ *If you want a certain career, affirm and admire the qualities that you need for that career that you see in others or in yourself, and bless those who seem to be at the place in their careers where you want to be.*

✓ *If you want a stronger connection to Nature, praise it or care for it in some specific way.*

✓ *If you want increased health, bless everyone and everything that you encounter that is healthy.*

✓ *If you want a better relationship, feel admiration for and bless those who already have one.*

✓ *If you want increased confidence, boost someone else's, and aspire to be like those that have it by blessing yourself.*

✓ *If you want a deeper spiritual connection, bless beauty, tranquility, and Nature.*

✓ *If you want more happiness, bless goodness and the potentials for goodness in people and Nature.*

Despite its simplicity, blessing is powerful beyond measure; issuing forth from and through you the very qualities and attributes that anyone would most wish to create for themselves and for others. Aloha is powerful medicine, and by continually filling your mind with it, you attune to, and strengthen the creative force that is within you. This creative force is called *Mana* (pronounced Muh-Nuh), which is the sixth principle of Huna, and it teaches that each and every one of us possesses all the power of the entire universe!

CHAPTER NINE

ALL POWER COMES FROM WITHIN

Mana: Divine, supernatural, or miraculous power, authority, or privilege.

Throughout Polynesia, folktales and myths abound that tell of the miraculous exploits of the powerful and audacious god *Maui*. He is considered a master shaman, capable of shape-shifting into other forms (birds being his preferred disguise), and accomplishing a host of other marvelous, extraordinary feats. As a demi-god, both divine and mortal, Maui has distinctly human traits as well, for he can be clumsy, mistake-ridden, lustful, ambitious, and childlike. Because he has often found pleasure in behaving outside societal expectations, Maui's feats have earned him a reputation in the South Pacific as less of a divine being to be revered, and more as a popular cultural hero.

There are many versions of the Maui legends, originating from Hawaii, New Zealand, Fiji, Samoa, and Tahiti. Despite differences in some details, all agree that Maui's adventures and accomplishments have had lasting impacts on all humans and Nature. Mana, or creative power, as it relates to the sixth principle of Huna, is exemplified in the imaginative, co-creative efforts of this trickster deity, and it is for this reason that I want to share a few of Maui's legends here.

It is said that during an ancient era, the sky was oppressively close to the ground. The clouds blocked much of the light, which not only caused great darkness, but also made everyone have to bend over and crawl around, constantly bumping into one other. Even the tops of the trees were flattened by the sky's great weight. When Maui went to visit a local Kahuna to seek a solution, the old, wise man tattooed a magical symbol on Maui's forearm and told him that it would give him great power. Maui then came upon a beautiful Polynesian maiden who knew that he was a master shaman, and asked him to use his power to lift up the sky. Maui flirtatiously told her that if she allowed him to "drink from her gourd" (innuendo implied), it would give him the strength that he needed to lift up the sky. The maiden gave Maui an elixir whose effect, not to mention the effects of whatever other intimacies transpired between the two, was so strengthening and enlivening that he used his enhanced vigor to push the sky upward, far past the highest mountains, and lifted its edges over the vast ocean, placing the sky where it remains today.

But while the people were enjoying the new light and space under the sky, there came another problem. Maui's mother, Hina, was frustrated by how little work she could accomplish in the shortness of the day, for the sun's passage across the sky happened far too quickly. As any obedient son would, Maui sought to remedy the situation. Using a net that he made from the enchanted hairs of his sister (also named Hina), he captured the sun, tied it to a tree, and threatened to give it a good thrashing with his magical stone ax. Then he facilitated a skillful negotiation with the sun, asking it to slow down its daily journey. The sun finally agreed, and Maui smugly went back to his awestruck mother, pointed upward and said, "You're welcome!" We're still benefiting from the long days of sunlight from that fateful agreement.

As the youngest of five brothers, all of whom were named Maui (which must have made for a confusing household), the god Maui was ridiculed and teased by the other four Mauis. The brothers accused him of being a rather ineffective and lazy fisherman, so they would leave him at home on most of their Saturday fishing trips. Determined to prove them wrong, Maui went to the underworld to visit his half-alive, half-dead grandmother named Murirangawhenua, who gave him her jawbone (from her dead half!) to use as a magical fishhook, known as the *manaiakalani*, or "the hook from heaven." Maui then gathered a few of his mother's flock of 'alae birds to use as bait, and off he went across the open ocean, on an outrigger canoe, taking his four siblings with him, intent on claiming the title of an accomplished fisherman. Maui dropped his hook into the deep blue waters, and his line suddenly grew taut. The manaiakalani snared what seemed to be an enormous catch, and after a long and arduous struggle, Maui reeled in the entirety of the Hawaiian Islands from the depths—the very islands that still exist today.

After repeatedly rejecting the romantic advances of a giant eel named Kuna Loa, Maui's mother found herself in danger of drowning. The lovelorn sea serpent had created a dam that funneled the tidewaters into her cave dwelling, intending to drown her, along with her family, for having refusing his affections. Fortunately, Maui arrived on the scene, magical ax in hand. With one great blow, he destroyed the dam, saving his clan. Next, a high-speed chase between the demi-god and the eel ensued in water and on land. Traps were set, and Maui finally caught Kuna Loa and took great delight in hacking the villainous serpent into many tiny pieces. The pieces were scattered into the sea, transmuting themselves into the numerous species of fish, both great and small, that still live around the islands. On the very site where Maui buried the great eel's head, the first palm tree sprouted, bearing a new creation: coconuts.

After so many daring and amazing feats, Maui decided to pursue the ultimate prize—immortality—not only for himself, but for all beings. "Death," he said, "is degrading and an insult to the dignity of man." Maui wanted to eradicate death by stealing the heart of the goblin goddess Hinenuitepo, who was responsible for bringing death to all creatures when their time came. Maui's plan was to crawl inside the goddess's body as she slept, steal her heart, and return a piece of it to all humankind, ensuring their immortality. How he got there is unclear, but once Maui was inside Hinenuitepo's body, the 'anea birds that he brought with him as companions on this journey made a chirping sound that awakened the goddess, who immediately crushed and killed Maui outright. Maui's death may be his most important lesson for humanity: His failure implies that immortality for us isn't appropriate; otherwise, he most certainly would have succeeded.

Maui clearly knew how to make things happen. He was a master of Mana, the innate power that each of us possesses, that special quality that enables us to generate life however we choose, and to empower others to do the same. The Maui stories teach us about ourselves, for just as Maui was capable of fantastic deeds, we are no different. The sixth Huna principle, Mana, states that there is nothing outside us that is more powerful than we are, and there is nothing that can't be touched by our influence. Every dynamic action that we take contains an inner spark of universal power that spans the galaxies and beyond. Not only do we have this power, but so does everyone and everything else, equally and without exception. We exist in an infinitely powerful universe, and that powerful infinitude converges at the point that we each call "myself": *All power comes from within.*

We looked at many of the qualities of Mana in the section on Hawaiian magic in Chapter Two, so I won't reiterate them here. But at the same time, I hope that it's abundantly clear from our exploration of Huna and the seven principles thus far that the power to create our life comes from each of us individually, and the more health, entitlement, positivity, and expansiveness that we possess, the more Mana is available to us to accomplish whatever it is that we desire. Another meaning of Mana is "authority," which implies the right to exercise power or author our lives as we see fit. This is our Mana in action.

At the heart of the cultivating that which brings us Mana is the building of our self-esteem, for nothing takes us farther away from the truth about ourselves—and the power we each possess—than the all-too-common belief that we ourselves are something other than God. We are all sparks of God, and if there is an ultimate purpose to our human lives, it is in our individual realization of this truth. If everyone could only see themselves clearly, the Trappist monk Thomas Merton wrote, "We would fall down and worship each other." This isn't necessarily hyperbolic, for the power that Huna's sixth principle refers to is divine power, and every time we think ourselves as being capable of anything less, we diminish the precious opportunity to see the miracle of our potential.

Self-esteem isn't just about feeling good about ourselves, and it certainly isn't egotistical; it's about holding ourselves as the precious beings that we are, with the full awareness that if the universe didn't need us, we wouldn't be here. That being so, we are to cherish ourselves by developing the gifts that each of us possess so that we can share them with the world. The nineteenth-century Hawaiian Queen Kapiolani had a favorite motto, *E kūlia i ka nu'u,* which means, "Strive to reach the highest summit." The more we value ourselves through our own self-investment, the more Mana we claim for ourselves.

When a shaman is doing shamanic healing, he or she is essentially performing two simple actions: removing that which obscures power or restoring power that has been lost. That's all there is to it: taking out or putting back in. But the shaman can only do this successfully if the client utilizes the power inside themselves to accept the power back, or to release that which blocks it. In other words, any effect— positive or negative—that another person has on you can only come about if the power within you grants and allows it. *All power comes from within, and each of us has all of it.*

Maui couldn't really make the sun do anything it didn't want to do. The power within the sun chose to agree to his request, and by doing so, the sun granted itself the opportunity to experience much more of itself by creating longer days in which to shine. Nor did Maui have the strength to lift the sky by himself; it was the sky's inner authority that allowed itself to be lifted, and the sky grew to its vast expanse in the process. The Hawaiian Islands used Maui's fishhook as an opportunity to be brought to the surface so that they could finally exist in all their splendor, and the unborn sea creatures and coconuts of the world utilized the slaughter of the giant eel as the chance to birth themselves into being. Even the specter of death utilized Maui's attempt to assassinate it as an opportunity to teach the world that death is inevitable, and need not be feared.

Exemplified in the stories of Maui is the true definition of power, which is *to influence others toward their empowerment.* Real power is present in our ability to *em*power. In Hawaiian, the word *manamana* means "to empower" or "to impart Mana." True power is never power *over* something, because that implies retaliation and fear, which cause power to dwindle, and power *against* something only causes resistance. But when we use our Mana to empower others, we further creation and growth. This, as we've discussed, is the energy of the forest: If we get back to the energy of the forest, then we get back to Nature, and if we are back to Nature, then we are back to God, and this is why all power comes from within, because nothing lies outside of God, including you.

Now, if we are all-powerful, Godlike beings, then it seems a rather steep and dramatic fall from grace when we contemplate how often we don't come close to thinking of ourselves in this way. True empowerment seems almost impossible in this age of social media, where personal validation comes in the forms of "likes," "followers," and "swipes to the left"; where advertising and consumerism are in a constant, frenzied race to sell you whatever will alleviate what you fundamentally and surely lack; and where society, family, and government remind you continually of your insignificance. And the "powers that be" (notice what I just called them) want it that way, because if you stay small by worshipping at their altar, then you remain beholden to *their* whims.

Just as energy flows where attention goes (Huna's third principle), the converse is also true: *Attention flows where energy goes.* Because so many of us pay so much attention to the opinions of the external power structures (such as media, family, and society in general), those structures have been energetically loaded with the clout and authority to tell us who we are, and how we are supposed to be. In fact, the power structures often have more Mana than we do because we give our Mana away to them.

"What will they think of me?" is a pandemic concern in our culture, and for good reason, for we are psychologically wired to give our authority away to the external world. In Sigmund Freud's psychoanalytic theory, which includes the Id and the Ego, the last agency of the human personality to develop is the Superego, our self-critical conscience, or inner-critic. The Superego has nothing to do with our own autonomy, but instead reflects the standards of society, cultural rules and norms, and the opinions of perceived authority figures like parents, teachers, and even those who we might consider the "popular crowd." Like a petulant teenager, the Superego only cares about what everyone else thinks, it is often judgmental and immature, and is devoid of any spiritual outlook whatsoever. It holds us to idealized standards of perfection of which we can't help but fall short, and it vacillates between a polarized sense of self that is either totally amazing and legitimate, or completely terrible and illegitimate.

It isn't that the Superego is entirely "bad." It's great for things like learning proper table manners, dressing ourselves appropriately for certain events, and keeping us going to the gym in order to look trim and attractive (and anything else that helps us to adhere to and fit in with societal expectations), but isn't good for much more than that.

Because the Superego is only interested in that which is outside of us, its standards and judgments are often in direct opposition to our true feelings, our unique perspective, and our essential nature. From a shamanic cosmological standpoint, there is nothing even remotely equivalent to the Superego, so to practice Huna is to live in a paradigm where the Superego doesn't exist.

You'll know if your Superego is in charge if you consider the standards and opinions of others to matter more than your own. If this is the case, then you allow too much of your power to lie outside you, which makes it next to impossible to honor Huna's sixth principle. The shaman's mind answers only to itself, and *doesn't care in the slightest what anyone else thinks.* I myself witness no greater relief, and nothing feels to me more like I am watching someone step into "adulthood," than when a client decides to relegate their Superego to its proper place by claiming their own authority with the insistence that the decision to legitimize themselves is solely theirs to make. The Hawaiians have a great word that indicates how we might rid ourselves of our overdeveloped Superego: *paulele,* which means "faith" or "trust," as well as "Stop jumping around!"

Self-esteem, self-reliance, and inner empowerment are the greatest gifts that you can give yourself. Developing them is among the most spiritual of practices, because it allows you to honor the God within you that God always intended you to be. Every time you forgive yourself, give yourself the benefit of the doubt, tell yourself that you can do something, bless your life, say yes to your dreams, enrich yourself with learning, legitimize your feelings, empower another, or eat healthy food you are increasing the Mana that you possess. The power of the entire universe exists within you, and the ultimate task of your lifetime is to build a sense of self that knows it and believes it.

Mana Practice — The Permission Plumeria Meditation

When I was studying with a shaman in the mountains of the Chapada Diamantina in Brazil, he taught me something about the human energetic field or aura (*hoaka* in Hawaiian) that I will never forget. He said, "You have your body and the three feet around it. That is yours to do with as you wish. Let the universe have everything else." In other words, because all power is within, we alone decide what we chose to hold in our personal space—nothing outside our energy need enter without our agreement, and nothing can influence us unless we choose to be influenced by it. Everything has all the power (just as we do), and we acknowledge this by giving everything, including ourselves, full permission to have it.

Boundaries are a tricky concept. Implied in our need to create them is our need to protect ourselves from something. Because of Huna's third principle—Energy flows where attention goes—every time we use boundaries with protection in mind, we attract more of what we fear by reinforcing it with our focus. In this exercise, rather than intending protection, we are creating boundaries that are permissive and agreed upon by all parties involved.

I call the following meditation the Permission Plumeria. It's a great way build your inner authority and create personal boundaries. Because we are constantly being influenced by and receiving feedback from the outside world, it can often be difficult to maintain our autonomy and sense of self—we aren't always sure where we end and others begin, or what is energetically us and what is the energy of another.

This meditation is best done while having it read to you by someone else while you follow along with your inner awareness. Alternatively, if you are working alone, you may wish to record it, and play it back.

Begin sitting in an upright position with your back straight but comfortable. Feel your feet on the floor. Be aware of the support of the cushion that you are sitting on, and of the Earth beneath you. Feel yourself sitting in your body, and feel the solidity of your body. If the body is the temple, then you are sitting in the temple. Become gently aware of your breathing, and allow yourself a few conscious inhales and exhales. When you feel relaxed but still quite alert, allow yourself to breathe, and on your next breath, allow your eyes to close.

With your eyes closed, notice if you have, in any way, left your body. If so, come back fully into it. Feel yourself sitting in your body. Find your heartbeat inside your chest, wrists, armpit, or groin. Sense the aliveness inside of you: tingling, pulsating, changes in temperature, aches, or soreness. You are simply becoming aware of your body, and the aliveness inside your body.

Breathe.

Now, become aware of your skin in all directions. That outermost layer of you—the front, back, and sides of you. Feel where the skin of your legs touches your pants or your skirt, and become aware of the skin of your face, on the back of your neck, and on your scalp. Feel the skin of your torso, your arms, your hands, and the tops and bottoms of your feet. For a few breaths, feel your skin in all directions.

With your inner awareness, and with your feeling or kinesthetic sense, from every point of your skin, begin to extend your consciousness outside your skin for one half inch in all directions—one half inch out from your face, torso, arms, legs, and feet. Don't forget a half inch behind you as well. Find that space just off your skin in all directions. Notice that although you are now feeling the space that is outside of your body, it still very much feels like you—it is your energy, your aliveness. It is outside of you, but it is still unmistakably you.

Breathe.

Now, from that half-inch point outside you, surrounding you in all directions, begin to extend your consciousness and your awareness further outward until it seems to dissipate or feel fuzzy and unspecific. You're now allowing your inner vision and your feeling sense to extend itself outward until it no longer feels like you anymore. Generally, this is about a foot and a half, maybe two feet, outside of you.

Now, bring your awareness back just enough to where you can find your space, and your energy again. With your intention and imagination, create a crisply delineated boundary around yourself in all directions. You will notice that as you do this, while still very much sitting in your body, that you are now surrounded by an egg-like structure, or a bubble. This is your aura, or in Hawaiian, your hoaka. This is the personal space that is only yours. Affirm for yourself that you have complete sovereignty over it. You alone decide what happens in your aura, and who, or what, is allowed to be there. You have absolute dominion over your space.

Breathe.

Notice where you are in your aura. Are you off to one side of it? In the back of it? Or the front? Just notice, and be curious. See if you can adjust it so that you are right in the center of it, so that the bubble surrounding you is even and symmetrical all around you. You are still sitting in your body, but also aware of the energy all around you that has a distinct boundary, and you are sitting in the middle of it. It doesn't need to be a hard or a severe boundary, just something to help your awareness perceive what is your personal energy field, and what is outside of it.

Now, right in front of you, at about your heart's height, at the edge of your aura, create a beautiful Plumeria flower, and let it hover there. A Plumeria is usually white with light pink or yellow shading, and beautifully fragrant. Your flower doesn't have to be a Plumeria; any flower will do. Allow your inner vision and your imagination to create a Plumeria (or another flower), and place it at the edge of your aura. Let it float there in front of you.

*Your Plumeria can move at the edge of your aura in any direction.
It can move to the side, above you, behind you, or below you, but it
always remains at that delineated boundary of your aura. See with
your mind's eye or feel with your inner awareness your flower's ability
to move at the edge of your aura.*

*Now, we are going to "program" that flower with an intention, we
are going to give it a specific instruction—and we are going to set your
flower at the intention of "permission." Anything outside your aura,
anything on the other side of your Plumeria, has full permission to have
its experience, while anything within your aura, anything between your
body and your Plumeria, has full permission to be your experience.*

*Any energy or experience that is directed at you from the outside
world will go into the flower first, and you will maintain all the space
on your side of the flower until you decide what you want to do with
the energy or experience that has been directed at you. So, no matter
what is coming at you from outside your space, it will move first into
the flower, which can move in any direction to catch it. Then, you can
decide what to do with it, as you maintain that foot-and-a-half space
around you in all directions.*

*Everything—the entire universe on the other side of your flower—has
full permission to have its own experience, while everything on the
inside of your aura has full permission to be your experience.*

*You don't need to "become" the energy that is coming at you, and
you don't need to merge with it. Instead, it moves first into the flower,
and you then have the space and the authority to do whatever you like
with the energy that has come at you from the outside world. Another
way to say this is that you are directing everything outside of you, to
"Talk to my Plumeria first."*

*Now, imagine a typical morning at home or maybe at work. Notice
who is around you, or whom you might be interacting with. Allow your
Permission Plumeria to be in place and functional—hovering and mov-
able at the edge of your aura between you and whomever you are with.*

Whatever energy or information that comes at you from other people will first move into the flower. You have permission to have your experience inside your space behind the flower, and everyone else has permission to have theirs on the other side of your flower. Picture a typical morning interaction with someone with your Permission Plumeria in the space between you and them.

Now, bring to mind a time when someone approached you with anger or with fear. In your mind's eye, see someone approaching you who is either angry or fearful about something. Allow your Permission Plumeria to be there. Now the other person's fear or anger goes into the flower first—then you get to choose how you are going to handle their fear or anger, while the other person has permission to have the experience of their fear or anger.

Also, notice that you can absolutely feel and understand the other person, and you can clearly see that they are fearful or angry. Maintaining your own boundary doesn't mean that you can't empathize with the other person. But you have that space of a few feet around you that is just for you, and you can do with it whatever you choose; you can decide what can enter it, and what can't.

In a moment, you will be ending this mediation, and you will be opening your eyes. Before you do, feel yourself sitting in your body, fully aware of your aura, that personal space around you that is all yours. Let your Permission Plumeria be with you, hovering in front of you, but free to move anywhere around the edge of your space. Keep the flower there even after you open your eyes, invoke it whenever you wish, and set the intention that it will continue to represent "permission": You have permission to have your experience, and everything else has permission to have its own experience. You have all the power to decide what you want your experience to be, and everything else has all the power to decide theirs.

Now, slowly open your eyes and relax.

You may wish to record your experience of this meditation in your journal.

You will find that the more that you work with it, the Permission Plumeria is an extremely effective tool for strengthening your boundaries and maintaining your personal energy field. It affirms your Mana by reminding you that your power comes from inside you, and that you have complete sovereignty over yourself. In a class I was taking with him, Serge Kahili King said that he never allows himself to be disappointed by anyone. "People will always do what they are going to do," he explained. Nothing is more empowering than giving yourself the authority to grant everyone the right to be exactly as they are, including yourself.

The seventh Huna principle, Pono, comes at the perfect time in our journey through the principles, because in knowing that we have all the power in the universe within us to create whatever we choose, we need some sort of barometer that can help to tell us if we are on the right track. And that something comes in form of a question: *Did it work?*

CHAPTER TEN

EFFECTIVENESS IS THE MEASURE OF TRUTH

Pono: Goodness, true condition of Nature, right, beneficial, accurate, correct.

Some years ago, a client came to me with severe pain and tension in her neck. She had been to doctors and specialists, massage and physical therapists, and she had even gone through an excruciating medical process of having long, surgical needles stuck in her neck in order, I guess, to release the fascia tissue there. This was all to no avail; no matter what she tried, nothing offered her any relief.

During our first session together, she shared her symptoms with me. I surmised that this wasn't really a physical problem but was actually an energetic one. I told her this, and suggested that we try some energy work. "Energy work isn't real," she said rather angrily. "I am not in the least bit spiritual. I don't believe in any of that, I think it's all hooey, and if I had known that this is what you did, I never would have come!"

In that moment, I realized that because she had been referred to me by one of her friends and had not seen any of my online materials.

She did not know that I am an energy healer, but must have imagined that I was some sort of specialized massage therapist. I told her that she was free to leave, of course, but since she was already in my office, why not give some energy work a try?

I did some hands-on healing, after which she reluctantly admitted that her neck did feel a little better, and I told her that I thought it would continue to improve over the next few days. About a week later, she called me again. Just as angrily as in our first exchange, she pointedly told me that she now had no pain at all. She begrudgingly told me she wanted to schedule a follow-up session, but that she believed that the entire reason why her condition improved was because of "the placebo effect."

After she arrived for her next appointment, and despite the marked improvement, she told me that she thought that I was "full of it," that I was some sort of "snake oil salesman," and that I was probably playing "mind games" with her. I said that whether she liked me or not or believed in what I did made no difference to me as long as her condition improved. If she didn't want to change her beliefs, who was I to tell her that she should? Attributing her success to the placebo effect was working just fine for her! We had one more session afterward, and I never heard from her again. However, around six months later, I learned that the work we had done together had impacted her so much that she was referring her friends to me.

The seventh principle of Huna is Pono. It speaks of practicality and flexibility, thumbing its nose at the "rules" by equating veracity with results. Pono teaches us that there is no right way to do anything, no system that is better than any other, no preferred methodology, correct path, appropriate process, or single approach. *All that matters is what works.* The shaman's mind considers only that which is useful to be of interest, and it determines the legitimacy and the validity of any action not by following procedural standards, established paradigms, or even specific beliefs, but solely by the successful outcome that the action achieves: *Effectiveness is the measure of truth.*

Truth is a relative term, not an absolute one. "Absolute truth" doesn't exist, because everything, including Huna, is simply something that someone made up. But truth isn't just random either, for when we produce change or cause things to happen that we want to happen, the specific reality to which we individually subscribe is verified. We decide what is true by how well abiding by that truth works for us. Because all power comes from within, truth is an entirely subjective experience, and like everything else in Huna, only you can decide what truth is for you.

My client couldn't deny that our work together was effective, but because the world is what she thought it is, she had to contextualize it to fit into her reality of placebos and mind games. Whether it was the result of magical energy or psychological manipulation, her neck stopped hurting, and that was all that mattered.

Being Pono means that we are "right" with ourselves; Pono is a felt sense of equanimity, balance, and harmony. We reach this healed state because the actions that we take to get us there are of the same quality of "rightness" as the results that they produce. In other words, we achieve Pono by the rightness of the means, and those means are unique to each of us. Recalling that Aloha is the only ethic in Huna, we must also consider that the results that are truly productive (as well as the means of achieving those results) are those that increase love and happiness. For instance, if we become rich and successful by stealing from others, or by working ourselves into illness, then we aren't actually being effective, which means that we are not in alignment with the seventh principle.

The shaman's skill lies in his or her ability to shape-shift into whatever those who seek healing need them to be. The shaman has many different methods, processes, and approaches available and, as the ultimate utilitarian, he or she will choose whichever is of the most practical and the most useful intervention under the circumstances. In my private practice, on any given day I may do gentle energy healing, be brutally confrontational, teach a Tantric breathing practice, do Ho'oponopono, speak of Jungian theory, or be almost entirely silent and just hold space and listen. Pono implies a willingness to leave no stone unturned until we find what uniquely and rightly brings each of us to equanimity and balance.

I recently watched computational biologist Eran Segal's TED Talk, "The Perfect Diet for Humans." I was intrigued by its title, because there are so many different theories on eating and weight control, and I was excited about the possibility of a definitive answer: Would the "perfect diet" be high fat, low fat, low carb, high protein, keto, or paleo?

Along with other scientists and clinical dieticians from Israel, Segal conducted an extensive study of the effects of eating certain foods on blood glucose levels. (A major contributing factor in gaining weight are the spikes in our blood glucose levels after we eat a meal.) Monitoring thousands of people over many weeks, and testing hundreds of different foods, from tacos to Brussels sprouts, the study found that while some foods caused glucose levels to rise in some people they had no effect, or even a reverse effect, on others. Genetics, lifestyle choices, geography, age, sex, and the presence of innumerable species of bacterial and microbial organisms that live in our gut, were all factors influencing the observation that certain foods had deleterious effects on some people, but not others. The study noted that the healthiest meal plan for some people included foods like pizza, ice cream, and cookies, while for others these should be strictly forbidden. And it concluded that the "perfect diet for humans" is so highly individual that it can only be determined on a case-by-case basis. The findings of Segal's study demonstrate the essence of Huna's seventh principle: It is only through seeing our differences that we find what is most individually valid.

To take one hundred percent responsibility for ourselves is to discover and align with our own unique truth and to develop the autonomy to recognize what isn't true for us. Nowhere is this more important than in our spiritual lives. There is an old Zen *koan*, or riddle, that says, "If you meet the Buddha on the side of the road, kill him." This is a warning to be wary of spiritual teachers or leaders who claim to have definitive answers, or who claim themselves to be more enlightened than you or anyone else. It also warns us to beware of any spiritual path that hints at its superiority over others. Nothing outside of us is necessarily real, and encountering a "Buddha" who is other than you may cause you to fool yourself into thinking that another's truth is more legitimate than your own. The Hawaiian proverb, *Ho'a'e ka 'ike he'enalu i ka hokua o ka 'ale* means: "Show your knowledge of surfing on the back of the wave." There may be many who talk a good game, but what is actually real is proven only by the outcome.

Close to twenty years ago, I was visiting Sedona, Arizona, for a Reiki training, and while I was there I wanted to meet some of the local healers for which Sedona is famous. I had an amazing healing session with Jeffrey Allen, a powerful energy healer and teacher whose work has had a lasting impact on me. We took a liking to each other, and decided to go hiking together the next day in the Sedona mountains. Although I was in the midst of a Reiki training, the healing that I'd had the day before with him had been unlike anything I had ever experienced. I wanted to know what he did, how he did it, and where I could learn it.

Jeffrey shared some of his background and training with me. But as he described his process, things weren't quite adding up for me, because he didn't reference a modality that he had ever formally learned. He said he was studying daily with "ascended masters and spirit guides via meditation" who were teaching him his ways of working. It eventually became clear to me that through years of trial and error, Jeffrey (and whoever Jeffrey was working with) had created his

own methods from scratch. In the same way that Mikao Usui had discovered (or rediscovered) Reiki energy and the process for teaching it
to others, which I had gone to Sedona to learn, Jeffrey had also channeled his own healing system into being. He had essentially made the
whole thing up, and it was every bit as effective as anything else. This
was an important lesson for me, and one that I hope you will take
from the seventh principle: The right way for you is only *through* you.
If it works, then it's true, and if it's true, then it's considered Huna.

But what if it isn't working? To that I say, "Mahalo to the Seven
Principles." When whatever you are trying to create is not coming
to fruition, you simply need to go back through the principles again
and adjust your process until you get the results that you want. When
things are not happening as you would like them to, the shaman's
mind reminds you that:

1. Because the world is what you think it is, you can change your
    beliefs or choose to think something else, which then can't
    help but change the world. (Ike)
2. Because there are no limits, you can know that anything is pos-
    sible, if you can figure out how to do it. (Kala)
3. Because energy flows where attention goes, you can adjust,
    change, or intensify your focus. (Makia)
4. Because now is the moment of power, you access your power
    by making yourself fully present in the moment. (Manawa)
5. Because love is to be happy with, you can prioritize happi-
    ness and increase love's presence in your actions and your
    thoughts. (Aloha)
6. Because all power comes from within, you can rely on the
    infinite power inside of you. (Mana)
7. Pono: Because effectiveness is the measure of truth, you can
    increase your flexibility, and try something else until a solu-
    tion appears. (Pono)

Pono Practice — Hailona

For thousands of years, indigenous cultures and magical practitioners have been using stones, shells, and bones, to gain insight or information through the occult means of divination. More recently, cards, dice, and runes have been used, particularly in the Western world. *Hailona* is a Hawaiian word that means "divination," "casting," or "throwing dice." The following is a simple practice of lithomancy, or divination with stones, that comes from the Kahili family tradition. It allows you to use your intuition and your creative imagination in relation to the seven principles of Huna to solve problems, or to gain insight into them.

You will need seven fingernail-sized stones (all seven should easily fit into your clenched hand). Because you will be tossing the stones, albeit gently, make sure that the stones that you choose are not too delicate or too easily chipped—they could be semi-precious stones, crystals, or even flat marbles. Each stone should be a different color, with each color corresponding to one of the seven principles, as follows:

1. White or Clear – Ike: The world is what you think it is.
2. Red – Kala: There are no limits.
3. Orange – Makia: Energy flows where attention goes.
4. Yellow – Manawa: Now is the moment of power.
5. Green – Aloha: To love is to be happy with.
6. Blue – Mana: All power comes from within.
7. Purple – Pono: Effectiveness is the measure of truth.

The kaona (hidden meanings) in the word *hailona* reveals much about the process:

Ha means "breath" or "energy." We begin the process of hailona with a few pikopiko breaths: Focus your awareness on your navel as you inhale, focus your awareness on the crown of your head as you exhale, and then repeat this process a few times. Pikopiko breathing helps us center ourselves, and builds our energy or Mana before we start the process of Hailona.

I means "to affirm" or "state an intent." Choose something in your life for which you would like help or advice. It could be something that you would like to create, or a situation or an issue for which you would like insight. In a moment, you will cast the stones, and receive advice from them on the subject you have chosen.

Lo means "to obtain." You will now cast your stones to get your answer. While holding all seven stones in your closed hand, focus on the subject of your inquiry. You can move the stones around in your hand or jiggle them however you like. Then, when you feel ready, gently toss them on the ground or a flat surface. The white stone is considered the *Kumu* or "foundation stone," and you will get your answer—the principle that you most need to consider—by observing whichever stone has landed closest to the *Kumu*. For instance, if the red stone is nearest to the white stone, then *Kala* is the main consideration for you; if the green stone is nearest to the white stone, then *Aloha* is the path to your answer.

Na, as you know from the word *Huna*, means "calm," or "pacified," and it also has an interpretive meaning: "The serene state after a healing." After you cast the stones and receive your answer, allow yourself to relax into a state of contemplation as you interpret your answer (see the Color Guide below). Assume that whatever advice that you have received from the stones is significant, and if considered appropriately, will bring insight and healing.

If two or more stones land very near the white stone, this may indicate that two or more principles are influential. And any stones that are quite far away from the white stone may indicate that their corresponding principles are not a factor at all. Let your intuition guide you. If anything about the way in which your stones have landed seems noteworthy (they may even form a picture, image, or symbol of some kind), or makes you curious, allow that to be part of your interpretation.

Because we have not yet addressed the psychic powers of the unconscious body-mind, which some Hawaiian traditions call the *Ku* (and which will cause you to toss the stones in such a way as to receive the perfect answer), simply trust that whatever you receive from the stones is the most applicable advice for you at this time. From a Huna perspective, the stones' answer simply can't be wrong.

Color Guide

This color guide will help you interpret the stones' guidance.

WHITE (Ike): Because we use this stone as the Kumu or foundational stone, we don't interpret from it, except to say that the interpretation itself utilizes this principle. Ike is about the *thinking mind*, and when we consider the stone nearest to it (i.e. the answer or insight that you are seeking in the form of one of the principles), our mind will engage, because the very nature of guidance or advice is to encourage us to think differently or to adjust our beliefs. In this way, Ike is always present when we practice Hailona.

RED (Kala): If the stone that represents this principle is nearest to the white stone, you are being asked to look at *limitations, boundaries, and tension.* What is constricted, or in the way of what you want to create? Is this constriction internal within you? Or is it external, in the outside world? What impedes your freedom? What minimizes the vision that you have for yourself in regards to the subject you asked about? Where are there limitations? What do that those limitations look like: Do you see fear, doubt, cynicism, stress, financial concerns, rules, or social constructs?

ORANGE (Makia): If the stone symbolizing this principle is nearest to the white stone, you are being asked to look at your *focus and attention.* Are you giving enough focus and attention to what you want to create? Are distraction, lethargy, or confusion preventing you from focusing? Do you give up too easily? Are there life circumstances, habits, or limiting beliefs that get in the way of you giving attention on what is important to you? How can you increase your attention and focus? Is there inner conflict that keeps you from focusing? How can you give a more concerted effort to what you want to create?

YELLOW (Manawa): If the stone that represents this principle is nearest to the white stone, you are being asked to look at *presence.* Are you grounded and centered in the present moment? Do worries or fears take you away from being in the now? Are you procrastinating or putting things off until another time? Are there things that you know that you should address but which you chronically avoid? What behaviors and habits take you away from being present? What kind of present moment do you often create for yourself? Do you self-annihilate, create fear, clamp down on your feelings, or somehow avoid what is happening?

GREEN (Aloha): If the stone representing this principle is nearest to the white stone, you are being asked to look at *love and happiness.* As you consider what it is that you want to create, what needs loving attention? Are you critical or judgmental of yourself or others? How can you increase happiness as part of your process? Do you bless the things you want, or those people who have already attained it? Do your thoughts about what you want to create habitually veer toward the positive or the negative polarity? In what ways can you bring more love to this issue?

BLUE (Mana): If the stone symbolizing this principle is nearest to the white stone, you are being asked to look at *personal power.* Do you have the self-esteem that can support what you want to create? Do you follow other people's rules or authority more than your own? Are you self-reliant? Are you confident or doubtful? Charismatic or shameful? What can you do to strengthen your resolve, and increase the faith that you have in yourself? Do you consider yourself a victim to outside circumstances? Do you need to invest in yourself in some way—education, gaining a new skill, improving your health?

PURPLE (Pono): If the stone representing this principle is nearest to the white stone, you are being asked to look at *flexibility and creativity.* Is there another way or means for achieving what you want to create? Do you roll with the punches, or are you stuck in your ways? Have you tried the same thing over and over without successful results? Are you following someone else's ideas or rules about how to achieve results? Do you need to create a new game plan? Are your current beliefs working for you in substantive ways? Is there a new path, teacher, methodology, or approach that may be more right for you?

Not all of the promptings in this color guide will necessarily apply to any single answer, so I encourage you to create your own, using each principle as a template. You may also start to allow your intuitive knowing to be part of this process by using the richly textured themes of each of the seven principles as a point of entry into your own intimate, contemplative practice. Simply cast the stones, read them by observing the colored stones' proximities to the white stone, and then allow your own creative and imaginative knowing to emerge.

Once you get more familiar with the colors and their correspondences with the Huna principles, you may choose to hold gently your white stone and your colored "answer" stone close to or touching your Na'au, the area right below your navel, and see if any other insights present themselves, or if the stones start talking or communicating with you. That's something a shaman might do.

Now that we have reached the end of our exploration of the seven principles of Huna, it is up to you to utilize these ancient ideas by bringing them into your everyday awareness. When passing on esoteric or cultural wisdom, a Hawaiian might say, *He mau makana nâu kêia na kô mâkou kûpuna,* which means "These are the gifts for you from our elders." The seven principles are, indeed, a special offering from the ancient ones. With awareness (Ike), freedom (Kala), focus (Makia), presence (Manawa), love (Aloha), confidence (Mana), and flexibility (Pono), there is nothing under the sun that you can't reach and accomplish, and no height of imagination beyond which you cannot explore. As you continue to work with the principles, you will find that layers upon layers of meaning and possibility will keep revealing themselves to you.

PART THREE

The THREE SELVES

The Greek philosopher Socrates offered the universal directive, "Know thyself," but in Huna we expand this directive to: "Know *all parts* of thyself." Huna wisdom teaches us that we can harness untapped potential, skills, and effectiveness by recognizing disparate and hidden aspects of the self, bringing them into awareness, and learning to harmonize them. Through the examination of the three fundamental selves, or innate powers, which we each possess, you will discover that you are far more that you ever imagined. To *know thyself* is to know that you have the ability to unite all that you are into a powerful and complete new totality.

For millennia, psychological, philosophical, and spiritual systems have sought to dissect and organize the many complexities of the self. The overarching conclusion is a three-fold conception of humankind: We are, separately and together, body, mind, and spirit. The sixth-century B.C. mathematician and philosopher

Pythagoras was probably the first Western thinker to formulate this framework of the self, citing what he called the three *Principas*, or physical, mental, and spiritual aspects of the human being. His influence is clearly felt in Sigmund Freud's psychological model of the Id, Ego, and Superego (although Freud's system bypassed the spiritual aspect entirely), as well as in Carl Jung's model of the conscious, unconscious, and superconscious minds.

The triune nature of all humanity is also found in many indigenous cultures and occult traditions. For example, members of the Lakota tribe of North America believe in a physical self (*woniya*), a mental self (*nagi*), and a transpersonal or divine self (*nagila*). The native Inuit peoples consider that they have three "souls": one that births itself with the first breath of life; another that is based on one's name and persona; and a third, immortal soul that is carried across lifetimes. According to the Feri tradition of Wicca (whose founders, Victor and Cora Anderson, claimed that it was heavily influenced by Hawaiian spiritual traditions and language), every human is said to possess the "fetch," which refers to a body-mind; the "talking self," or the mind that thinks and communicates; and a spiritual aspect called the "god-self."

The concept of three aspects of the self exists in the Huna system as well, and although it has many similarities to the traditions cited here, what emerges from Huna's concept of three selves is a uniquely shamanic paradigm of human consciousness, one that combines Nature, imagination, intellect, intuition, spirit, soul and the physical body.

In Hawaiian thought, the three selves, or aspects of consciousness, are named after the gods that are affiliated with the powers that each self possesses. The god

Ku is associated with all things physical, such as war, athletics, commerce, and artisanry, and Ku is the name of the unconscious body-mind. *Lono* is the god associated with the conscious thinking mind and is also considered to be the god of intellectual pursuits such as medicine, music, and agriculture. The god of high places and of creation is *Kane*, who represents our spirit, or the superconscious mind. While these names are associated with ancient Hawaiian legend and religion, the "three selves" of Huna is not a religious concept, but rather a philosophical and spiritual one.

Given that we are multidimensional beings, dividing the self into three, thirty, or even thirty thousand parts is, in and of itself, somewhat arbitrary. The second principle of Huna states, "There are no limits," which means that, from a Huna perspective, we think of separation merely as an illusion that is sometimes useful to consider. We separate the self into three aspects only for the purpose of gaining insight and understanding. In the same way that the heart, spleen, and liver cannot function independently from one another, neither can any individual aspect of our consciousness.

The ultimate goal that we hope to achieve by practicing Huna is the powerful synthesis of all three aspects. When Ku, Lono, and Kane are masterfully brought together, the result is called *Kanaloa*, which is the name of the magnificent god of the ocean whose inhalation and exhalation is said to create the tides. The powerful unity of all three aspects comes about through a deep understanding of them individually. Let's begin with the illusive unconscious mind, or the Ku.

CHAPTER ELEVEN

KU

As you read this paragraph, take a moment to notice the aliveness within your body. Turn your mind's eye and your feeling sense inward, and tune in to all of the internal processes that are happening inside of you right now: Your stomach is digesting food, your ears are attuning to peripheral sounds, your hands are holding this book steady, your lymph glands are secreting fluids, your eyes are imperceptibly moving back and forth as they follow the words on this page, the neurons in your brain are activating, and a part of you is assessing the frame of reference from your past experience that allows what you're reading to make sense to you. All of these things are happening with absolutely no assistance from that being you call "John Smith" or "Debra Jones." You intended to sit down to read this book, and you've chosen to focus on the ideas presented within it, and (hopefully) to comprehend them, while another part of you is engaged in seemingly innumerable other tasks. This part is Ku.

Ku is the unconscious body-mind. But "unconscious" is actually a misleading term, because as the part of you that oversees every aspect of your aliveness—from the beating of your heart, to the growing of your fingernails, to your digestion, hearing, sight, and mobility—your Ku never sleeps. Ku is only "unconscious" in the sense that we are largely unaware of all that it does, and all that it contains.

Your conscious mind (Lono), which is the aspect of you that you would most associate with your identity, may form a mental intention to walk from here to there, answer your phone, or brush your teeth, and your Ku is the part of you that actually does the walking by moving your legs and swinging your arms, engages your hands and fingers to pick up your phone, and maneuvers your arm from side to side across your teeth while tensing your fingers around a toothbrush.

"You" don't actually have the slightest idea how to do any of these things. You "know" absolutely nothing of which neurological synapses to fire, which specific muscles or tendons to engage, how to regulate your equilibrium, or how to utilize the proper amount of oxygen in your blood necessary to accomplish any of these tasks. But your Ku, as "the mind of the body," does. You simply form an intention—or rather, your conscious mind, Lono does—and your Ku carries it out. In this way, you might think of the Ku as a faithful servant.

Ku learned what it knows through its primary tool, which is memory. The Ku remembers things. First, there is the genetic memory stored in your DNA—you came into this world with genetic imprints that already held the programming for beating your heart, maintaining your body temperature and so on, and your innate artistic abilities, or your propensity for athletics, are likewise implanted in the biological and ancestral memory of the Ku. Then there is the learned memory that we acquire throughout our lifetime, a log of all that we experience. Learned memory may or may not be "correct"—we have been taught (and memorized) that a green light means "go" and that stealing is "bad," but we may have also learned that good girls don't have sex before marriage, or that only Christians go to heaven.

Although Ku, Lono, and Kane are specific to the Kahili tradition, some Hawaiian traditions refer to the unconscious mind as *unihipili*, a word that is often used synonymously with Ku which means "the spirit of a dead person believed to be present in the bones or hair of the deceased and kept lovingly," it also has a general meaning of "little one" and "little creature." These meanings infer both an embedded memory that is literally bone deep in our genetic and ancestral lines, as well as the memorized patterns, based on what we experience as children, that we learn to follow with obedience and consistency. Memory patterns, whether genetic or learned, are held within the Ku.

As a database for your memories, Ku always does its best to use what it knows to please you and to act in your best interest. But like a computer, it can only access information that has previously been stored in it, and if any of the information that it contains is "incorrect," Ku can seem to have its own covert agendas. This is why we sometimes do detrimental things to ourselves while being fully aware that they are not good for us. Throughout its life, Ku learned (and memorized) what is pleasurable and also what hurts, and its primary motivation is to continually seek out what it has come to understand is pleasurable and to avoid what it has come to understand is unpleasant.

For instance, as you read these words, this material might seem boring or too heady for your Ku, and your Ku might be nudging you to get up and have a snack, go for a smoke, or take a little nap. These activities might be more agreeable and pleasurable for your Ku than continuing to read a book on Shamanism, and Lono, your conscious mind, can either choose to keep reading and ignore the feelings and sensations of sleepiness, hunger, or nicotine withdrawal, or succumb to them. Whatever you decide is just fine (although I must remind you that smoking isn't good for you); what is noteworthy is the recognition that your Ku and your Lono can often be at odds with each other. Your conscious mind may wish to read further, but your unconscious mind may have other motivations that would be more pleasurable for it.

Ku communicates through emotions and feelings, and if Lono, the conscious mind, is paying attention, it has the option to respond to them, or not. If you decide to continue reading, you might discover that I suddenly decide to tell you a terrifying ghost story, or share something emotionally painful with you about abuse from my childhood, or preach to you about the superiority of my political beliefs. If your Ku has experienced anything similar in the past to what I have just shared—and would therefore have automatic opinions and reactions to those opinions—it would produce an emotion or feeling that your Lono would then decide to act on: You could turn on a light or call a comforting friend if the ghost story scared you, reach out to your therapist if you are triggered by hearing about my abuse, or write me a pointed email if you angrily disagree with my political beliefs. Based on its history of pleasure and pain, Ku scans the environment for what it considers important, and then sends signals through feelings and emotions that enlist the conscious attention of Lono to react to them.

The memories that Ku prioritizes are those with the highest sensory impact, because they made the biggest impression on it. If someone has experienced active combat in the military, they may have a heightened and adverse emotional reaction to being in a crowded subway or a noisy restaurant, while another person without that experience would be relatively unaffected. Someone else may break into a cold sweat when asked to speak before a group of people, because they have a past memory of a parent or teacher humiliating them in front of others. An action film about violent mobsters may be a fun, adrenaline rush for those with no personal experience with criminality, but it may elicit feelings of shame, anxiety, or fear for victims of crime or past perpetrators of it.

The Ku primarily remembers whatever made it feel the most intensely, and since it is unable to distinguish past, present, or future, it follows that when a certain memory pattern is triggered, the intensity of the feeling in the present moment will be more or less comparable to what the Ku originally experienced when the memory was created. If you take a moment right now to bring to mind a difficult event from your past as vividly as you can, you will almost immediately feel the emotions of that event in your body. Conversely, a pleasant memory will spontaneously elicit positive feelings. Try it.

I have previously discussed the importance of feeling your feelings, acknowledging your emotions, and becoming aware of your mental habits, because these are all ways in which we actually pay attention to the Ku. From the standpoint of healing and growth, nothing is more important, because this is how we start to see the entrenched patterns from the past that no longer serve us—patterns which, if we are to heal or release them, can only be changed with the help of Lono, our conscious mind.

As a child, if your speaking up would have led to punishment or abuse, it may have been self-protective for you to remain silent and not express yourself, but when you became an adult, the voicelessness that your Ku memorized is a detriment, and our conscious awareness of this pattern is the first step in addressing it. When you watched Mom and Dad arguing viciously over money, your Ku memorized a pattern of equating money with problems and strife, and unless it is given another option, money will always have an emotional trigger. And if your Ku learned to soothe anxiety or fear through overeating or indulging in substances, then using food or substances as coping mechanisms will become a memorized pattern that will persist until Lono makes the decision to change something, and attend to the anxiety or fear differently.

In many of his writings, Max Freedom Long referred to the unconscious mind as the "low self." This is not meant to indicate lesser importance, but rather that the unconscious mind serves and follows the directives of others. Ku, more than anything, is like a child, in its most active stage of development in childhood. Children are largely blank slates—they are in a constant process of learning who they are and what the world is, based on what how they are treated, what they experience, and what they are taught.

Just like children, Ku takes personally everything that happens to it, and it memorizes who it is on the basis of whatever it experiences: If the child is hit, the child learns that something about them is bad enough to be "hit-worthy," and if the child is ignored the child learns that they don't really matter. Likewise, if a child is told repeatedly that they are not "good enough," they will learn that there is something "wrong" with them. The ancient Hawaiians were so sensitive to the impressionability of children that when a woman learned she was *hapai*, meaning pregnant, both parents would make a concerted effort to protect the unborn child by refraining from engaging in negative thoughts and emotions during the pregnancy and even by singing and talking lovingly to it.

Children lack the autonomy and the critical intellect to understand that what happens to them isn't necessarily about them, so if they are mistreated, neglected, or misunderstood, they will conclude that they are at fault and lay the blame entirely on themselves. The child makes sense of his or her world by assuming that there is a reason why they have been treated in such and such way, or why they have experienced whatever they have, and that "reason" is the result of something about them. Abuse, mistreatment, neglect, and indifference wreak havoc on the development of a child's sense of self, and Ku develops a "mistaken identity" that becomes as automatic and ingrained as any of the natural processes of the body. Although memories themselves may be long forgotten, the Ku holds an imprint of them all, and it will habitually respond based on what it knows itself to be.

Without guidance, the Ku will think and do the same thing over and over again unless it is taught something different. The conscious mind, Lono, provides that guidance. What the Ku does well, it does very well, and when Lono encourages and blesses it, the Ku wants to do even better. But when Ku struggles, it is because it holds beliefs and opinions, accepted as true at some earlier point in its life, that once caused fear, unhappiness, or limitation. When Lono takes the time and effort to reparent Ku by guiding it to release, reinterpret, or change its misunderstandings of reality, Ku and Lono move into a powerfully congruent partnership.

In Chapter Four, when you identified your negative core beliefs and changed them to their positive opposites, I was actually asking you to look first at the habitual impediments unconsciously held within your Ku and then use your Lono to consciously shift them and attend to them differently. The first principle of Huna states, "The world is what you think it is," and unless you deal with those things that your Ku has memorized that are not beneficial for you, the problematic beliefs that Ku holds will more than likely eventually actualize. How vital the agreement of the unconscious and conscious minds is for health, healing, and living successfully cannot be overstated and, as you will see, this allegiance is also what brings us into alignment with God.

The shaman's mind always seeks to find the root cause or the underlying basis of a problem, since getting at it directly is the easiest way to remedy it. When someone comes to me for healing, they are almost always needing help in addressing longstanding patterns that have occurred repeatedly throughout their entire lifetime: They *always* choose the wrong type of man, they *always* have money issues, they are *always* unable to finish what they start, they *always* isolate themselves from others, they are *always* in and out of addictive behaviors, and so on.

These recurring dynamics are not character flaws or personal failings, they are entrenched patterns that were learned in childhood, and are now embedded in the Ku. Although the person may have memorized these unhelpful ways of being as a child, perhaps decades earlier, that child is never far away, because the child's memory patterns are, quite literally, held within the physical body. Alice Miller, psychotherapist and author of *The Drama of the Gifted Child: The Search for the True Self*, writes:

> The truth of our childhood is stored up in our body. And although we can repress it, we can never alter it. Our intellect can be deceived, our feelings manipulated, our conceptions confused or our body tricked with medication. But someday our body will present its bill. For it is as incorruptible as a child, who, still whole in spirit will accept no compromises or excuses. And, it will not stop tormenting us, until we stop evading the truth.

Ku memory lives in the body, and it is often connected with the area of the body that was most highly activated when the memory was occurring. When a child is told not to speak, they learn to constrict their throat or jaw. When they are taught that they are not allowed to feel their feelings, or that their feelings don't matter, they tense around their lower belly. When they discover that their world is unsafe, or they come to the conclusion that they are "unlovable," they tighten the space around their heart for protection. These become areas of chronic tension that could be anywhere in the body, and because the Ku can neither act of its own accord nor create its own solutions, these constrictive patterns will remain unless Ku is taught something different by the conscious mind. Remember that, from a Huna perspective, all physical illness or emotional dis-ease (*ma'i* in Hawaiian), is born of tension, and healing (*ola*) occurs when Ku is guided to release the constrictions that it has placed on itself.

I recently had a client who was a young, good-looking man in his late twenties. His physique was stocky with hard muscle, and he was clearly an amateur body-builder. He told me that he had been feeling depressed for some time; also, despite his youth and excellent health, he complained of a barely functioning libido. He was the son of Middle-Eastern immigrants, and his family owned a liquor store that was, in his words, a "goldmine." As the eldest son, he was expected to run the family business and support his entire family in the future. For as long as he could remember, his father had worked ceaselessly, never taking a break, a vacation, or a sick day; in fact, the young man said, even on the day his paternal grandmother died, his father worked in the store.

Since birth, this young man had been groomed to follow in his father's footsteps. Not only did his father not support his desire to attend college or allow him to apply, but he also did not take seriously any of his son's interests in music, poetry, and language. And, as if all of this wasn't already enough, the young man's marriage had been prearranged to a woman whom he had never met.

This young man's muscular physique was his Ku's armor. He had closed down on his voice, his heart, his feelings, and his genitals. The only way he could maintain such a chronic state of self-denial was through extreme tension, and he had packed on layers of thick muscle to toughen himself up.

Within just a few moments of placing my hands on his torso to do some energy healing, he had an intense release of sadness and rage. In that moment, his Ku allowed itself the opportunity to release the longstanding and imprisoning lock-down that had been imposed on it. Remember, Ku needs guidance from the conscious mind; in this case, that guidance came through the gentle touch of my hands. As the young man allowed his body to soften, the truth of his situation revealed itself more fully to him. At the end of our session he said that although he now understood the nature of his problem, and felt a sense of relief that he hadn't experienced in years, he knew that the chronic tension would undoubtedly return because, as he told me sadly, "My family will always come first."

Ku oversees the physical body, and in the same way that we attend to our feelings and emotions in order to overcome our detrimental mental and emotional habits, our physical health can be addressed in exactly the same way. Let's say you are in a job that you despise, one in which you feel deeply troubled and compromised, and you choose to do nothing about it. Perhaps your Ku has learned from memory that it can get out of doing certain things by getting sick or having an accident of some kind. Because Ku's primary directive is toward pleasure and away from pain, it might create an illness or unconsciously organize an accident that would keep you from going to work.

Remember the clients I told you about in Chapter Two, who would manifest accidents and obstacles to keep them from making it to my office? This is the same dynamic at play. Their Ku didn't even want them to go through the temporary pain and discomfort of addressing their problems, or making difficult life changes, and it created all kinds of ways to avoid them. Getting hurt, having an accident, or becoming ill may not be pleasant, but if Ku perceives that these situations are a better option than going to that awful job—or that uncomfortable and invasive visit to the healer—then that is exactly what the Ku will do.

Physical illness and accidents are Ku's attempt to solve a problem that the conscious mind has refused to solve. According to Huna, everything that happens to us is created by our thoughts, both conscious and unconscious. When we don't acknowledge the unconscious language of the body—our feelings and emotions—we defer to the learned memory of Ku, which often has the limited understanding of a child, to make decisions for us.

Notwithstanding what I have shared with you so far, I do not want to imply that Ku is entirely problematic. Although Ku may hold memories and habits that aren't advantageous, it can also be responsible for some of our greatest gifts. When I describe what Ku can actually do for you, besides its extraordinary ability to keep you alive, you will yearn even more to learn how to let go of the negative patterns that it holds—even though these patterns have often been chosen unconsciously by a six-year-old! With attention and love, we can remove the obstacles that eclipse Ku's magnificence.

Our Ku wants us to grow, and it is linked to the universal human urge toward growth. We have previously discussed the energy of the forest, or nature, as an unstoppable force of growth and creation. When we align with that force, we discover the path that reveals our soul's journey. Ku is a rudder, a directional apparatus that prompts us, through our feelings and emotions, toward that creative force. I have advised you that the best way to discern your life's direction is to identify and pursue that which feels loving, enriching, and expansive, and to avoid all of that which doesn't. Ku provides the necessary sensory feedback to help track this.

Ku not only provides us with the wisdom of our emotions, but another kind of wisdom as well, one that allows us to know what we cannot know, and to see what isn't there: Ku is the source of our intuition. The ancient Hawaiians, and all indigenous peoples, did not believe that access to intuitive or psychic ability was granted only to a few special and gifted initiates; they were certain that these are natural propensities that all humans possess.

As we have discussed, the Ku can hold onto belief patterns that don't serve us. One prevalent belief is that intuition, precognition, clairvoyance, and psychic sight are unreal or simply impossible. All too often we have been taught by other people's Lonos—because our own Lono wasn't developed enough at the time to put a stop to it— that such abilities don't actually exist. Therefore, many of us have not claimed our innate, intuitive gifts, but if we allow ourselves to do so, we will find that *we are brimming over with them.* In fact, the vast majority of what is taught in today's classes and trainings on intuition and psychic ability is not so much about skills or methods, but about learning to trust the intuitive "hits" or psychic "downloads" that we receive.

Remember, in Chapter Ten, in the section on Hailona, or stone casting, I said that if you toss the stones with a clear intention, it would be impossible for you to get the wrong answer. Why? B*ecause Ku does the tossing, and Ku is the seat of our psychic ability.*

Ku *is* the unconscious mind, which means that it is also connected to what Carl Jung called the collective unconscious mind, which means Ku has the capacity to know just about everything about everything. For instance, when doing divination by casting stones, Ku already knows and understands the question, and how best to answer it. Ku will pick up the stones and hold them in just the right way; cause tiny micromovements in your hand, palm, wrist, and fingers, which will place the stones in the perfect configuration; and release them at the precise moment with the exact force and velocity necessary to bring you the correct answer. And when you shuffle Tarot cards, hold a pendulum and watch its movements, cast runes, or scry tea leaves, the same dynamic takes place: The Ku psychically organizes the answer. Any divinatory tool is a means through which the Ku communicates the astonishing information that it already possesses.

Ku is an amazing part of you. While the unconscious mind may hold unhelpful patterns, Ku also has access to unbelievable wisdom. Practicing Huna means that your conscious mind must not only address Ku's problematic aspects, but also respond to and honor its gifts—the very same way that you would treat a child. Every child has gifts that need acknowledgment and cultivation, and in order for them to truly flourish, they also need loving guidance and protection (which comes from Lono).

Before we scrutinize Lono, the conscious mind, in the next chapter, let's take time to work with Ku experientially.

Ku Practice — Kummunication, or Dialoging with the Body

The shaman's animistic mind sees everything as alive, conscious, and wanting to connect, and this includes the physical body. I was first introduced to the practice of engaging the body in conversation while training in Cherokee Bodywork with Dr. Lewis Mehl Medrona.

Serge Kahili King teaches a Huna practice that is practically identical, and I have also seen similar methods practiced in Central and South America.

In this practice, you will learn to communicate directly with Ku. As we've discussed, the Ku holds memories as energetic and muscular imprints in the body. This practice explores those hidden patterns so that we can find out what purpose that they serve, where they came from, what they are trying to tell us, and how we can best relate to them.

You may want to read through this exercise before doing it, or you may choose to record it so that you can play it back and follow along as with a guided meditation. Either way, I also recommend that you leave a bit of open space where I have prompted you to "Breathe," so that you have can expand deeply into the practice. We tend to ignore, or are largely unaware of the Ku; here, we relate to it directly and invite it to engage with us.

You can do this practice either sitting or lying down.

Begin by allowing yourself to relax and to go inward. Close your eyes, and take a few conscious breaths. Breathe in and be aware of it, then breathe out and be aware of it. As you breathe, feel yourself sitting or lying down inside your body. Your body is the temple, and you are inside of it. You might feel a sense of aliveness, tingling, temperature, even of pulsation inside your body; simply allow all of that to be there. Take a few moments to make deep inward contact with yourself.

Breathe.

Now, begin to focus on a part of your body that you are curious about or that you feel might need healing or attention. This could be an internal organ like your liver or lungs, or an external part of your body like an arm, shoulder, or foot. It could also be a more generalized area of your body, such as your chest, solar plexus, or lower belly; or you can choose a chakra, if you relate to chakras. Begin to make intimate contact with whichever part of your body you have chosen. Simply breathe, and feel into it for a few moments.

Breathe.

Next, I will prompt you with some questions that you will ask this part of your body, and you will simply wait for Ku to respond to them in whatever way it chooses. Allow plenty of spaciousness for whatever may arise. The answers may feel like they are coming to you in your own voice, or they may come in images or as intuitive messages. Just know that there is no right way to do this, so whatever surfaces for you is exactly what should be.

What are the physical sensations that you feel in this area of your body? Does this area of your body feel open or closed? Does it feel comfortable and familiar, or foreign and unfamiliar? Or something else? What emotions do you feel as you relate to this part of your body? What is the overall feeling impression that you receive from this area of your body?

Breathe.

What is the story that this part of your body is telling you? What is the dream that this part of your body is dreaming? Ask for a story or a dream that is related to this part of your body. It could be visual or auditory, or you may have a feeling sense about it. What does your Ku want you to know about this part of your body? If your Ku could speak, what would it tell you about this area of your body? Because there are no limits, trust that whatever you are seeing, sensing, or experiencing is in some way related to this part of your body.

Breathe.

Do you have a sense of when this story or dream first began? Does this feel like an old or recurring pattern? Is it connected to a memory or to memories from your past? Is it connected to a relationship with someone from your past?

Breathe.

What would a symbol or an image of this part of your body look like? Use your creative imagination to come up with a symbol or an image that would express this part of your body. Is it a bright sun? A dark room? A locked box? A tranquil lake? A clogged drain? Something else? Does this symbol or image mean anything to you, or make you feel a certain way? What is this image or symbol trying to convey to you?

Breathe.

Now, whatever you happen to be experiencing, assume that you are a shaman, and change the story, dream, or image of this part of your body. If you don't like it, change it to something that feels better or more satisfying. If you do like what is there, improve it in some way. Either way, take some time to do this.

Breathe.

When there is a mental satisfaction or a feeling of completion, begin to reorient yourself within the space around you. Slowly open your eyes.

As you come out of this experience, notice the part of your body that you have been focusing on. Has it changed in any way? What have you learned about it? How can you take care of it in a better way?

You may wish to jot down some notes on this experience in a journal.

Ku Practice — Ku Resistance

This is a very simple journaling practice that will help you to see the habitual negative patterns in your Ku. By becoming aware of the battle that sometimes goes on between your conscious and unconscious minds, you can begin to change or release what doesn't serve you.

In a journal, write down three or four things that you want to do, to be, or to have, within the next twelve months.

Once you have named these things, look at each one individually, and breathe a few conscious breaths. As you contemplate each thing, allow the strong, contrary voice to come up from inside you. This is that limiting and negative voice that often tells you, "No!" Let this voice tell

*you all the reasons why you can't or won't be able to do or have these
things. It may tell you why you don't deserve them. It may even tell you
all the reasons that it would not be good or beneficial for you to achieve
these things. Let this voice's opinions be fully expressed.*

Write down whatever this negative voice has told you.

*Whatever you have written down is representative of the entrenched
patterns, and the limiting beliefs, in your Ku.*

*As you contemplate each of these, ask yourself some questions about
them: Where does this negative belief come from? Does it sound similar in
tone or syntax to that of a parent or authority figure from your past? Do
you remember being taught or told something similar in your childhood?
Can you trace this thought form to a specific memory or memories? Does
this negative belief feel like something that you have held for a long
time? Is it trying to shield you from possible pain, discomfort, or shame?*

You have now begun the process of understanding the unconscious body-mind Ku. While Ku has incredible gifts, it can also hold
outdated, unhelpful memory patterns that will need guidance and
attention from the conscious mind, Lono, in order to change. Lono is
the mature, parental spirit within, and we will learn next how to use its
directive capabilities for healing, personal growth, and self-mastery.

CHAPTER TWELVE

LONO

Many choices have led you to this very moment. You have decided to read this book, which means that there is an essentially uncountable number of other things that you have decided *not* to do. In order for you to focus on these words, you must diminish your awareness of just about everything that is not them. Let's face it, if you wanted to, you could think about your toes, visualize a green hippopotamus, put this book down and recite a mantra, or search the internet for the best hotel in San Juan, Puerto Rico. But, for now, you have made the choice to place your attention on this page, you have formed an intention to read and learn about Huna, and you have an awareness that you are doing just that. The aspect of you that can do all of this is Lono, your conscious mind.

It is actually somewhat paradoxical to call this part of you "conscious" because, unlike the unconscious mind, and the higher self or superconscious mind (which we will address in the next section), your conscious mind goes to sleep every night, and it will eventually die. In his book *Kahuna of Light*, Hawaiian author Moke Kupihea observes that the conscious mind is not eternal, but "... has evolved solely to serve one's current existence ... once this life is done its consciousness will cease to exist." Lono is connected to your personality, who you outwardly think yourself to be in this lifetime, and it creates the "story" that is currently "you" through the choices that it makes. Because it is the link between the "hidden" wisdom of the unconscious mind and the higher wisdom of the superconscious mind, the Lono is one of the shaman's greatest tools, and the universal totality of you can be consciously expressed through it.

Lono makes decisions and choices, and it has the power to oversee and govern our lives. In many ways, it is responsible for our quality of life, because it has the ability to focus and take action on what it decides is most beneficial for us. It is our inner CEO: It can create its own rules about life, imagine reality however it pleases, and override difficulties and obstacles by forming creative solutions. Because it is the source of our focus and our attention (which, as you know from Huna's third principle, elicit the creative energy of the universe), Lono contributes greatly to the evolution of our life based on what it chooses to focus on with consistency, and the "strength" of our Lono depends on our individual capacity to sustain attention. The conscious mind *wills* things into being through its ability to hold steadfast awareness.

When functioning optimally, your Lono utilizes and supervises the intuitive, emotional, and sensory information that it receives from your Ku, and it addresses anything it finds held in your unconscious mind that is antithetical to your best interest. Lono guides Ku toward health and happiness and away from limitation and fear, and it is extremely sensitive to the directional whisperings of purpose and higher calling that come from the higher self (Kane). While Lono receives information and influence from these two sources, the conscious mind is not meant to take orders from them but, first and foremost, to follow its own directives. Ideally, Lono, the conscious mind, is in charge.

Other Hawaiian traditions, when referring to the conscious mind, use the word *uhane* rather than Lono. Uhane means "ghost" or "guiding spirit," but also connotes giving purposeful direction, and breaking down the syllables of the word Lono gives us further insight: *Lo* means "to achieve" and *Ono* means "desires." The conscious mind, with its powers of will, choice, and imagination, is the guiding force that helps us make things happen. Lono's primary motivation is resolution. It addresses conflict by determining the best course of action to take in order to bring every aspect of life to its best resolved and most agreeable conclusion.

While the conscious mind may seem quite familiar to you, I find that, for most people, it is generally underdeveloped, and its potential is far from fully realized. I have already likened Lono to a loving parent, and I can't overemphasize this analogy. A fundamental component of our healthy growth and development is the need for us to create a kind and learned authority within ourselves, a parental self that always has our best interest at heart; loves us unconditionally; and provides us with structure, support, and tireless attention. By elevating your conscious mind to this position of leadership, you can create a trusted friend and a wise advisor that you can always rely on.

For many of us, this kind of ideal parent was not modeled for us in our families of origin. Those who raised us may have been unwilling, unable, or simply unaware of the kind of meticulous care that is needed to truly do right by a child. And what exactly does it mean to do right by a child? *Nothing short of narcissistic indulgence of the child.* Children who receive effusively loving and constant attention don't grow up to be egomaniacs, they simply grow up to be okay with themselves, and they have far fewer problematic imprints in their Ku.

Many of us who were not parented appropriately did not learn to develop this ever-present and nurturing "inner adult" for ourselves, and without one, *the child will run the show.* I assure you that every time you sabotage yourself, choose an unhealthy relationship, engage in destructive behavior, refuse to make changes that you know would be good for you, or find yourself in recurring patterns of negativity, your Ku is holding more authority than your Lono. Or, to put it another way, your unconscious and habitual drives and wounds are in control, rather than your conscious mind, which can make choices, create solutions, and advocate on your behalf.

Your conscious mind has the ability to retrain your Ku to accept whatever new choices and possibilities it decides are best for you. This goes far beyond just helping Ku release the negativity that it holds. Lono is connected to the imagination, which means that it can guide Ku to accept (and memorize) any extraordinary existence that Lono might conceive.

How do you get your Lono to create an extraordinary existence for yourself? It starts with engaging your conscious mind in the perennial task of loving and even—I'll say it—*worshipping* yourself with constancy and meticulous thoroughness, from this moment onward and for the rest of your life. If you are a spark of the divine, as you most certainly are, then this isn't an egotistical or outlandish suggestion—it's the only appropriate one, because it is only by making the conscious choice to love ourselves fully, that we are able to heal anything that we subconsciously hold that was born of *unlove*.

Over time, your Ku will memorize the messages of love (and any other wise guidance) that your Lono is teaching it, so that love will become your conscious and your unconscious reality. And, if the world is what you consciously and unconsciously think it is, then it stands to reason that love will predominate in your world.

Think about it. You are the boss of you, and nobody else but you. If this book offers you anything of value, it is by showing you, in as many ways as possible, that there is absolutely no limit to what you can create, or who you can become. All it takes is the conscious choice to think thoughts that are beneficial, expansive, and loving, and to go to battle with any previous memorizations that aren't.

Imagine being a child and having a parent raise you in accordance with the seven principles of Huna, with your primary caregiver and strongest formative influence continually instilling in you that *what you think changes the world; you have infinite possibilities available to you; the energy of the universe responds to what you focus on; being in the moment aligns you with power; love and happiness can guide you in everything that you do; all the power in the entire universe is already within you; and when things don't go your way, no big deal, you can just try something else.* If you choose to, you can parent yourself in exactly the same way.

Parents are supposed to pay extremely close attention to their children, and if they are doing it right, they will leave nothing unattended if they can possibly help it. We all know how to do this, but we often don't do it for ourselves. If the child cries, we wipe their tears. If they are scared, we talk them out of it. If they are confused, we sit them down and help them get clear. If we sense that they are not feeling their feelings, we give them full permission to feel them. If they are ashamed, we buck them up with praise. If a bully called them "ugly" at school today, we march over to that school, child in hand, and, knowing that the child is watching, we advocate for them. With children, every blip on the screen is important, noted, and addressed; to practice Huna is to enlist your conscious mind into starting to pay that much attention to yourself.

This is not self-indulgence, this is how you start to see yourself as the god-being that you are. When you hear the commonplace directive to "love yourself," this is exactly what it means: Lono giving love and attention to Ku (and the practice of Ho'oponopono, outlined later in this book, is expressly for this purpose). The Lono that you want is the Lono of the loving parent. This is the Lono I am suggesting you create for yourself, because this is the kind of Lono that can bring you to your own paradise, to your own Hawaii.

The conscious mind is a hidden power, one that we often take for granted. But when we learn to use Lono as an *uhane*, or "guiding spirit" that oversees and leads us toward empowerment, growth, and love, then we can align with the unfathomable abundance that is waiting for us to unfold further into love so that we can fully receive all of its riches.

Lono Practice — Connecting with the Child

Ku and Lono are often at odds with each other. Remember that Ku cannot make its own creative choices, it can only carry out what it knows. If what the unconscious mind has memorized is now harmful to us, although it may have served a useful propose in the past, the conscious mind must lovingly reparent it, which is another way of saying that we create agreement and congruency between what Lono wants to happen, and what Ku will allow itself (based on what it has memorized) to believe should happen.

In the next practice, these two aspects meet and reconcile.

The propose of the following guided meditation is for you to travel back in time to learn about your child-self and, if the child agrees, to bring it back with you so that it can be taken care of in a new and better way from now on. This process might also help you understand what Ku the child memorized that is detrimental, and how Lono can help release it, as well as what Ku needs from you that you have previously withheld or not known to give. As you are guided back to different times in your life, you will see that while your life circumstances may have changed significantly, your habitual negative patterns are all related in some way, and can often be traced back to your earliest experiences.

As with the other guided practices, read the following exercise over thoroughly before you do it, or record it with your own voice for replaying, and allow some space at the end of each paragraph for you to have time to experience it.

Close your eyes, and take a few conscious breaths. Begin by allowing yourself to relax and go inward. Breathe in and be aware of it, and breathe out and be aware of it. Allow yourself to make deep, inward contact with yourself. We will be taking a deep dive into your life's journey, so allow yourself to be curious and to be open.

As you breathe, think of your current life circumstances, specifically something that you may be struggling with. I am going to ask you to sum up your current life struggles in one word. This word is a negative emotion that is something that you frequently feel, an unpleasant emotion that predominates in your life right now, and one which you wish that you could be rid of. Bring to mind the one word, the one negative emotion that you want to release. Some examples might be anger, doubt, fear, confusion, loneliness, or stress, but these are just examples. What is the one word, the one emotion that you would like to remove from yourself at this time in your life?

Now, in your mind's eye, with your inner vision, move backward in your life by about seven years. Don't get too hung up on the exact number of years, just some time approximately that long ago. Whatever is coming into your mind is exactly right. It could be memories about a relationship, your career, or some other life event. It could even be you on a typical day around that time. If the version of you from seven years ago could release a negative emotion in the form of one word, what would that word be? It could be the same word that you came up with before, or it could be a different word all together. What is this one word, the one emotion that you would like to remove from the "you" of seven years ago?

Now, move back another seven years. Again, don't worry about being too precise with the exact number of years. As you see or sense yourself about fourteen years ago, what events or memories are coming to mind? It might be something that happened to you, an addiction you suffered from, a relationship that you were in, or a specific life event. Whatever is presenting itself in your mind is what you should consider.

*If the version of "you" from that time in your life could release a nega-
tive emotion in the form of one word, what would that word be? Is it
the same one as one of your previous words, or is it a different word?*

*Now, go back still another seven years, and repeat the process once
more. This time, you'll move backward in time for a total of just over
two decades. See yourself there, and notice what about your life (an
event, a memory, a relationship) is coming up. What emotion, in the
form of one word, would this version of you like to release? Is this the
same word, or a different one again from the previous words?*

*Depending on how old you are, repeat the process again until you
get to your teenage self. You might find yourself in high school or remembering something about an old girlfriend or boyfriend, the dynamics in
your home life at that time, how you felt about yourself as a teenager, or
a significant life event. If your teenager could release one emotion in the
form of one word, what would that word be? Is this the same word, or
a different one from the previous others?*

*Next, go back as far as you can remember to a difficult event that hap-
pened in your childhood. You don't have to go directly into a bad memory; instead, find your child self a few minutes after this difficult event
occurred. The event may be something that happened that has always
bothered you, or something you haven't thought about in many years. Or
there may be more than one memory coming to mind, which is fine too.*

*According to Huna, there is no time or space. You are right back
there now, at the same time, and in the same place with your child, your
Ku, a few minutes after a difficult event.*

*See your child self. Notice where you are and, perhaps what you
were wearing. If it's hard to visualize, you can even recall a photo-
graph of yourself around that time. Sense who else is around you. If
you are indoors, who are the people in the other rooms? What is the
emotional tone of this place?*

*Look into the child's eyes. You are right there with your child self
now. What is the child's expression? What is this child feeling?*

If your child could identify one word, one emotion that you wish they didn't have to feel, what is the word? Children often don't know exactly what they are feeling, so you may have to help them find the word. Is this the same word, or a different one from the previous others?

Consider that this last word is related to all of the previous words that you have traced throughout your life so far; it is the seed of a long-standing entrenched pattern in your Ku. While life circumstances and the cast of characters of your life may have shifted many times, underneath it all is an underlying pattern that comes from the difficult emotion that you have identified with your child self.

Now, speak to this child. Introduce yourself to them. Let the child know that you have come back from the future to be with them. Let them see you all grown up, and alive and well.

Tell this child that whatever has just happened to them, whatever the difficult event they have just experienced, that they have done nothing wrong. Let the child know that they were always perfect and blameless, and even though what just happened is unfortunate or unfair, it is not their fault, and that they shouldn't take it on as anything having to do with them.

Tell the child, "We don't want to hold onto this as having anything to do with us; otherwise, we're going to carry it with us for our whole life. We want to see it for what it is, that it's not about us, and we want to let it go right now."

Take some time to do this.

Now, if there is anything else that you want to say to this child, any unfinished business, do that now. Take some time to do this.

Ask the child what he or she needs from you. How does the child need to be treated by you now? What does the child need you to do? If you get an answer from the child, make a promise that you will do whatever they say. Take some time here.

Now, see if the child wants to come with you. Let the child know that he or she can stay where they are, but if they want to, they can come with you. See if the child prefers to come with you, and watch what the child does. Take some time here.

If the child decides to come with you, grab on tight, and when you both are ready, say goodbye to this place together. Now gently come back into the room that you are currently in, and slowly open your eyes.

You may want to record your experience in a journal.

If the child has decided to come back with you, then you can assume that he or she thinks that they will be better cared for by you now than by whoever cared for them in the past. If the child hasn't returned with you, this may mean that you need to work on reestablishing some trust with your child self or address any disconnection that you might have with your body or your feelings. Many of the practices in this book can help you with that.

Ku is the most "permanent" part of you. It can be taught to memorize any reality that your conscious mind feeds it—including the magical and loving one epitomized in this book—and it will never veer from what it memorizes unless and until it is taught something else. As a constant beacon of consciousness, one that never sleeps, Ku perpetually transmits to the universe whatever it believes about reality. With consistent guidance from Lono, Ku's beliefs can be transformed in such a way that they send out the very signals of consciousness that would invite the highest gifts of Spirit into our lives.

Kane, the higher self, spiritual self, and superconscious mind, is the aspect of us that has direct access to God, and it best acts on your behalf when Ku and Lono become more lovingly aligned. As you will learn in the next chapter, Kane takes its cue from the contents of both the conscious and unconscious minds, because it is through thoughts, and the intentions they hold, that we create a container in sympathetic resonance with the divine. This is how we attract divinity's gifts directly to us.

CHAPTER THIRTEEN
KANE

In ancient Hawaii, the ultimate god or Great Spirit wasn't a concept that the islanders could relate to—it was too big and too far away from them. They knew that the Absolute was there, and one look at their islands made it abundantly clear that it could rain down the highest Mana upon them. It wasn't that the islanders didn't understand the existence of a Supreme Being; they had many terms for it in their language, including the one that we will use: *Akua Nui* is used today to indicate the Christian concept of God, but for our purposes, can be thought of without any religious connotation as its literal translation, the "greatest god." The Hawaiians, like most indigenous cultures, didn't generally follow an ascendant model of reaching the ultimate divine—one that postulates that in order to find God, we must strive upward toward the heavens, and somehow transcend our worldly experience. Instead, they held the common shamanic viewpoint that we are not separate from God, because the divine is accessed through a natural part of the self.

According to Huna, we each have a third aspect of consciousness, the superconscious mind, called Kane, which acts as an intermediary between us and the spiritual forces of the universe. Kane is our personal god-self, our own individual creative source. Its main function is to take the content of what we hold in our mind and body and transmute it into material reality. Kane oversees the process of manifestation, the birthing of thought and intention into physical form.

The easiest way to understand this is as follows: Lono has an intention, and gives that intention consistent focus until Ku memorizes it as a fixed pattern. Once this pattern has been memorized by Ku, then Kane, in conjunction with the universe's highest spiritual forces, Akua Nui, brings that pattern into material existence.

Now, this is an extremely rudimentary explanation of the immensely complicated process of manifestation, but in order to utilize it for yourself, all you really need to know is that your conscious mind can make a choice to create something or to make something happen, and then you need to get your unconscious mind to agree with that choice—if for whatever reason it doesn't already. Once it does, your superconscious mind will say to God something like, "We have some serious congruency going on down here, so let's make this thing happen!" And bingo, it happens.

Kane shapes our lives in response to what we think and believe. In other words, Kane physically manifests the patterns that are held in Ku and Lono. Remember that the etheric aka substance is everywhere, all around us, and it contains infinite unrealized potential. That potential (aka) becomes actualized potential (mana) through our focus and attention (makia). Kane provides the spiritual magic that does the actualizing.

Some Hawaiian spiritual traditions know Kane as *aumakua*, and these words are often used interchangeably. Aumakua is the Hawaiian word for "ancestor," which implies that the superconscious mind is timeless. But aumakua's parts contain many seed meanings as well: *au* can mean "self" and "older," while *makua* means "parent" or "father." As you already know, the word *akua* means "a god or higher being," and *kua* means "high point of land," as well as "to carve things out of wood" or "to form things on an anvil." *Maku* means "to harden" and "to solidify," and *ma* translates as "by means of." If you put this all together, aumakua (or Kane) can be defined as *the ancient and wise higher self that is affiliated with the gods and creates our experience and manifests physical form.*

But Kane is not just the aspect of us that manifests or creates. It is connected to all of our ancestral lines, and holds within it all the data of our infinite soul material—all that we ever were, all that we are, and all that we will ever become. Kane is the home from which we each came from, and the storehouse that will receive us when we die. Even before you were born, your Kane placed you into that particular family, with those parents and that specific set of circumstances, in order to maximize your soul's growth during the incarnation that you are currently experiencing, with the hope that this time around, you might remember that you are God. *And the more difficult your path, the more likely you are to remember.*

The shaman's mind always considers challenges and suffering to be fodder for growth, because suffering provides us with an inner irritation that urges us to do whatever we must do to get better. In other words, our suffering puts us on the path to healing. True healing occurs when we are touched by the divine; when this happens, we discover that divinity itself is who we always were, and we can't help but want everyone else to discover this for themselves as well.

That is why ninety-five percent of my clients, once they have successfully completed much of their own healing, become healers themselves. They may not hang a shingle as a shamanic practitioner or an acupuncturist (although they might), but in some way they find themselves called to serve the collective sacredly, whether it be by writing a blog about the emotional intelligence of professional body builders, creating an exercise and wellness program for female divorcées, or starting a foundation for minority youth. Healing awakens the God within us, because God's influence was the reason why the healing occurred in the first place, and once you have been touched by God, you tend to hang around. Kane, then, holds our highest potential, and since we know that Buddhists believe that full enlightenment is possible in one lifetime, that is some great big potential.

The primary tool of Kane is inspiration. The superconscious mind inspires us to reach for and realize our potential. So even though I tend to emphasize the conscious mind Lono as the instigator of the process of manifestation, it should be noted that the Kane is often the initial inspiration that begins that process. When we are called in a particular direction, or we are inspired to take an action that might not seem to make sense or is contrary to the values with which we were raised but inexplicably excites us anyway, that is a sure sign that Kane has been activated. Harmony is the superconscious mind's primary motivation—our highest potential can only be reached by harmonizing the conflicting energies that we have within ourselves, and with the world. The more fully we realize our potential, the more we abide in harmoniousness.

You might think of Kane as your guardian angel, and many people experience it as such. Kane is an exceptionally loving being that wants the absolute best for you. It will silently cheerlead your triumphs; worry about your failures, protect you from danger; and send directional signals to you through synchronicities, signs, and omens that light your way. Although Kane is with us every second of our lives, it will seldom, if ever, interfere with our choices or with our free will. Kane tends to intervene only if we are veering wildly away from our potential or in serious danger of not realizing it. But when we are miraculously "saved" in a near-death experience, or we "accidentally" meet our life partner on a subway platform that we've never been on before because the line we usually take to work is closed for repairs one day, Kane has stepped in. But, while it may intercede in these ways, Kane generally follows your lead.

The imagination, which is Lono's domain, is one of the shaman's most important tools. Shamans use it to imagine what their clients could be like at the height of their wellness. But the shaman doesn't do this by just making something up that is "positive" for the client to aspire to—he or she reaches directly into the client's Kane, and is shown the potential that is already there. When I am doing counseling work, I often present clients with a new story or a future self that is infinitely better and far more appealing than anything they would conceive on their own.

Now, it would be highly unethical for me to get a client's hopes up about wonderful possibilities available to them if I didn't actually believe them myself. So, as my friends would tell you, although I am a relatively nice guy, I am not so nice that I just dream up rainbows and sparkles for people. I receive the information about a client's potential from their superconscious mind. They might react with excitement or fear—which are actually the exact same emotion, just with a different storyline—to what I share with them, but they never tell me that I'm wrong, or that they don't resonate with what I've told them. That's because the information didn't really come from me—it came from their Kane.

If you want to connect with the highest potential held in your Kane, simply imagine who you would be, and what your life would look like, if you were to become your most inspired self. Then make whatever you have imagined twice as good, and you'll be in the ballpark. In order to create that self, your Lono will make the choice to intend that self into being, and it will guide your Ku to lovingly replace or release any beliefs or habits that it holds that are antithetical to the creation of that new self. Your Ku will memorize this new pattern because your Lono has given it consistent focus, and then your Kane will automatically petition the highest spiritual and creative energies to bring that self into being.

A few years back, a female client in her late twenties came to my office. She was spirited and funny, joking a lot about her "messed-up life," and as she shared her story with me, I couldn't help but notice that she was at least a hundred pounds overweight. From childhood, she had always been inappropriately "used" by her family. She was a surrogate "therapist" to her father, who would talk to her about his money issues and the problems in his marriage; an impromptu "best friend" to her immature and insecure mother, who needed constant reassurance; and a "self-appointed parent" to her troubled younger brother.

Throughout her upbringing, she had learned to exist entirely for others, and to be whatever anyone else needed her to be: a receptacle for everyone's shirked responsibilities. As she grew older, her friends constantly exploited her and men toyed with her. Her boss at work was so emotionally abusive as to border on sadistic. The only way she could possibly hold everyone else's "junk" was to get bigger and bigger, which she manifested by putting on more and more weight. Her Ku had learned and memorized that this was who she was, this was how she was to be treated, this was what was expected of her—and to use food as a coping mechanism.

But she also had a secret. She had read Elizabeth Gilbert's best-selling book *Eat Pray Love*, in which the author told her own story of going on an extended vacation alone, finding her true self, and completely transforming her life. This young woman was greatly inspired by Gilbert's own story, which is another way of saying that the potential that her Kane held had been recognized and ignited, and her higher self had begun sending her directional signals toward realizing it. For the past two years she had been secretly saving as much money as she could so that she too could embark on a similar journey.

In her first session with me, she confessed that I was the first person that she had ever told about reading Gilbert's book, about the money she had saved, and about the vacation that she was thinking of taking. She also admitted that she was extremely conflicted about actually going, because, even though they weren't all that great, she would be leaving behind her job, her family, and her friends. It was all just too scary for her. She said she thought the whole idea was probably "stupid and selfish." She should really use those savings for something "sensible," such as retirement. It might be dangerous or lonely to travel by herself, and in any case, she was "much too fat" to go on a trip like this.

My client's Ku was riddled with fear and shame, and it couldn't support the potential of her Kane, for it had memorized a disempowered identity and a bleak and limited view of life that would never allow her to take that trip.

She came to me regularly for almost a full year. Each week, her Ku would present her fears, her worries, her low self-esteem, and anything else that would keep her from going on that journey. My Lono responded to everything she presented with a positive alternative and, over time, I was able to teach *her* Lono to do the same. I also told her that this trip would be the best thing that ever happened to her (because her Kane had already revealed this to me). Over and over again, our two conscious minds addressed every negative belief and self-limiting story that was held in her unconscious mind. Eventually, with steadfast focus from her Lono (and lots of guidance from mine), her Ku memorized a new pattern—one that was at least powerful enough for her to actually book her five-month, inner-quest vacation—the same vacation that was already held in her superconscious mind.

What were the actual results of that vacation? She was so fundamentally transformed that she decided to move to a new city, where she found a new apartment, started a new career as a life-coach, met a new boyfriend, attracted a new set of friends and, having lost all of her excess weight, she stepped into a new body. Kane had inspired her toward her potential, Lono had taught her Ku to memorize a new pattern that was congruent with that potential, and Kane had brought that potential into being.

The main reason why we are not more in communion with aumakua/Kane, or our higher self, is because we rarely, if ever, allow

ourselves to dream that big. We have all felt inspired to step into a lar-
gesse of self and an inspired life (Kane), but another part of us (Ku)
isn't strong enough to hold it (and may even be in direct opposition
to it), while yet another aspect of us (Lono) has not yet developed or
realized the powers of choice and focus that would get us there. This
is your work to do.

Kane is a being of wonderment, though not at all separate from
you. If we open ourselves to Kane's loving presence and the inspired
vision that it holds for us, we will discover the immensely good news
of who we truly are and what is possible for us, and we can use its
creative powers to bring forth a self that is far beyond what we could
imagine possible.

Kane Practice — Shamanic Journey to Kanehunamoku

You are about to embark on your first shamanic journey. In this
journey, you will meet and get to know Kane, your higher self, in
its dwelling place, which is called *Kanehunamoku*, or "Kane's hidden
island." Some Hawaiians recognize this fantastical spot as a floating island, or an illusory place that might exist in the clouds or in
another dimension altogether. Your Kane, of course, is already an
inseparable part of you, and you don't need to go on a journey to find
it. Kanehunamoku is only a metaphorical destination that we will visit
in order to engage with, and befriend, this highest spiritual aspect
of ourselves.

There is no correct way to engage in a shamanic journey. You might
"see" your journey in your mind's eye, or feel it kinesthetically in your
body. You might experience it by hearing a narrative or a story, or
you might have a different kind of experience altogether. You may
or may not have an actual visual experience that is similar to watching a movie. In my professional experience, most people don't. Over
time, you will become familiar with how you individually experience

shamanic journeys, but for now, trust whatever happens, however it reveals itself to you.

A shamanic journey is an entrance into the Po, the hidden worlds or "dreamtime" of the shaman's mind. This is where we gain access to spiritual intelligence, spirit guides, healing, mythical stories, and archetypical symbols. There is neither time nor distance in a shamanic journey—we can move deeply into the past or way out into the future, or visit faraway lands of the imagination. Don't think of journeying as something difficult to do, for it is nothing more than an intentional daydream that we enter with a childlike sense of play and curiosity.

Typically, you will begin each journey in a sacred place. This is a beautiful place in Nature that you may have visited before in real life, or this could be a place of the imagination. In the Hawaiian tradition, we call this place *Waena*, or "the garden," but the word also means "center" or "medial." The Waena is a kind of central hub for your journeys, a place from which you can travel anywhere in the mystical landscapes of the shaman's mind.

In many native cultures, although not in Polynesia, shamanic journeying is often accompanied by monotonous drumming (approximately two hundred and twenty beats per minute). I find the sound of drumming to be a helpful support, and there are many recorded drumming tracks available online that have been created expressly for this purpose. Drumming facilitates a light, trancelike state of awareness, together with a shift in brainwave frequency from the waking consciousness of the beta state to a theta state of deep relaxation. This is roughly equivalent to the consciousness of deep meditation, contemplative prayer, or that liminal state right before sleep. But if the drumming is not your thing, you may prefer to play some subtle metaphysical music (with no lyrics) or recorded Nature sounds to accompany you on your journey.

Shamanic journeying is most easily experienced while you are in in deep state of relaxation, though not so relaxed that you fall asleep, so allow yourself some time at the start to be in quiet receptiveness, and don't try too hard to make anything in particular happen. It can be helpful for you to lower the lights, cover your eyes with blindfold or a scarf, and lie down comfortably on your back.

Beginning journeyers often concern themselves with whether they are making up their journey in their heads, but this is an unnecessary worry. You may well find yourself making some of it up, but other aspects of it will spontaneously happen. Simply open your imagination to the intention of the journey—which, in this case, is to travel to Kanehunamoku to meet your Kane—and then let the journey do the rest. If you think you are making it up, just agree with yourself that you are, and keep going.

I encourage you to record the following text while speaking slowly, making sure that you pause at the end of each paragraph to allow yourself a little "dead space," which will give you enough time for your internal experience to develop fully when you replay the recording for your journey. Alternatively, you could read through the text several times, become as familiar as possible with it, and then simply prompt or guide yourself. Note that there is a section toward the end of the text during which you will want to spend at least ten minutes journeying without any guidance from the words.

Close your eyes, and allow yourself to relax. Feel the meeting points between the back of your body and the floor, or whatever you are lying or sitting on. Let your body be heavy. You might connect with the gentle tug of gravity on your body. Slowly scan your body, and as you do, release any tension that you might feel. Take a few moments to consciously soften and relax your body. Relax your mind as well. Let your breath be nice and soft, almost like a gentle inner massage, and feel your breath rise and fall in your chest and in your belly.

* * *

In a few moments, you will be moving into your Waena, your garden. This is a beautiful, sacred place in Nature. You may have experienced it before in real life, or it may be a completely imagined place. Remember that even though you may be imagining, hearing, or feeling your journey, you might not see anything visually. If you are unsure about this place, don't worry, for we will create it together.

Your Waena is not far from you; it lives right inside your heart. Now, begin to allow yourself to sink into it. Perhaps you see or feel yourself at the top of a beautiful spiral staircase that you will descend to reach this sacred place. Or, the entrance to your Waena may be a tunnel, cave, or some other kind of portal such as the roots of a tree, a doorway, or a waterfall. In whatever way is right for you, begin now, with your imagination and your feeling sense, to enter your garden. Breathe, and allow yourself to enter it.

* * *

Take a look around your Waena, noticing where you are and what is around you. This is a place of great beauty, safety, and sacredness. This place is just for you—every blade of grass and every drop of water is aware of your entrance into this place, and everything in this place loves you unconditionally. As you get to know your garden, notice that everything in it is alive and conscious. As you become aware of everything in your sacred place, everything within it will also become aware of you. Everything there is very pleased that you have decided to visit.

Are you in a meadow, a jungle, a pine forest? Are you on the side of a mountain, on a beach near the ocean, or in an actual garden? What is the sky like in this place? Is it daytime or is it nighttime? Is the sky cloudy or is it clear? What color blue is the sky?

What are you standing or sitting on: tall grasses, pine needles, sand, soil, or something else? What is around you? Notice whether there are plants or trees, or if there's a body of water. If there is a body of water, is it a stream, an ocean, a lake, or a river? What are the colors in your

sacred place? What is the quality of the light in this place? Notice every-
thing around you, and allow yourself to feel the beauty, safety, and
sacredness of this magical place.

Are there sounds in your place, of water or insects? Do you hear the
wind or a breeze? Maybe you can feel this breeze on your face or body.
On your next inhale, you may notice smells or fragrances in your place.
Are they smells of flowers, pine needles, sea-salt air, or the soil? Allow
yourself some time to take in every aspect of this place, luxuriate in its
sights, sounds, smells, and textures.

* * *

Now, feel your heart tug at you, gently propelling you to move in a
certain direction. You'll know the right way to go. Begin wandering
around your place for a bit, and eventually you will find yourself at the
opening of a path. This path may lead into a wooded forest, a dense
jungle, a beach, a mountainside, or somewhere else. Notice the size of
the path, and what the path is made of. Feel each step as you now begin
walking on the path. What is around you? Take it all in.

Soon, you will come to a clearing or an open space of some kind.
There is a being waiting there for you, a spirit guide to meet you and
accompany you on your journey. You may already know your guide, or
your guide could be unfamiliar to you. Your guide might be human
or in the form of an animal or an element of Nature. Or it might be
another kind of being, such as an angel, an ascended master, or an
ancestor. Become acquainted with this spirit guide, and know that this
being will help to take you to Kanehunamoku, Kane's secret island,
where you will meet your higher self.

* * *

Now allow this guide to somehow take you to a coastal shoreline,
from where you will be transported to Kanehunamoku. Your guide may
hold you as you travel, or maybe you ride on your guide's back as you are
flown over a vast ocean expanse. You may make the passage on a rainbow

or on a cloud, or there may be a vessel at the shoreline that will take you there over expansive waters. It might even be that your surroundings simply dissolve and fade away as you are somehow magically transported to the misty, mystical, and magical island of Kanehunamoku.

* * *

Up ahead of you, a group of clouds in the sky indicates the presence of an island. You are arriving there now. As you approach and begin to enter this place, you see that it is an enchanted isle, with sumptuous waterfalls and lush freshwater pools. There are gigantic, green mountains in the distance; there are glistening white sandy beaches that meet with deep blue, purple, and turquoise waters, and there are colorful coral reefs. There are verdant tropical rainforests, exotic birds, and jumping fish. This cloud-capped paradise sparkles with a heavenly energy, and a spiritual light pervades the air. Take in all the sights and sounds of Kanehunamoku.

* * *

It is on this enchanted island that you will meet your Kane. You may find that this being seems quite other than you, or it could be a familiar, although slightly different version of yourself. Simply be open to meeting your Kane in whatever way it presents itself.

Your Kane may show you who you would be at your greatest potential; the highest and brightest version of you that you could become. You might learn about your soul's true purpose, the ultimate reason why you have taken form in this lifetime, and you may in some way step into it. You might receive a message, an insight, or a vision of your destiny. Experience, merge, and connect with your Kane, your higher self, however it appears or reveals itself to you. Let it talk to you, guide you, or show you anything that you need to see or understand at this time. You can ask it questions, if you wish.

Spend at least ten minutes here with your Kane.

* * *

In a moment, we will be leaving this place, so it's time to say good-bye to Kanehunamoku for now. Give thanks or express gratitude in whatever way feels right for you—perhaps with a few words, or with a smile and a gentle bow. Hold this entire experience in your heart as you and your spirit guide retrace every step you have taken on this journey, going backwards until you arrive again in your Waena, your sacred place. In whatever way feels appropriate, thank your spirit guide and say goodbye for now.

* * *

Now that you've returned to your garden, find a cozy spot to rest and relax for a few moments, while this journey integrates within you. Ask yourself—how would my life have to change if I were to realize the potential that my Kane holds? What self-limiting beliefs, relationships, or stories are in the way of this attainment? What still needs healing in me? What needs my attention and my love? What actually matters most to me?

Now, find the staircase, the cave, the portal, or however you entered your Waena, and gently make your way back to the place where you started.

You may want to take some time to reflect on this experience with some notes in a journal.

Journeying to Kanehunamoku is just one way to experience your Kane, and Kanehunamoku is something that you can revisit whenever you wish and experience different results. But your Kane isn't just available to you while visiting an imaginative magical island. You are in direct contact with it every time that you appreciate beauty, bless the present moment, aspire to new possibilities, or engage in spiritual practice. Kane only wants to love you, to shower you with blessings, and to encourage you to reach for your deepest heart's yearnings. Kane wants you to go, to do, and to be. But it can have difficulty reaching you if you have not planted the seeds in your body and your mind that will grow and develop you into a vessel able to receive its spiritual riches.

The relationship between Ku and Lono defines the influence Kane can have on us. When all three of these aspects come together in agreement and in support of each other, we enter into the ecstasy of oneness and into freedom—a self devoid of conflict. This is Kanaloa, which I've mentioned is the Hawaiian name of the god of the sea. But Kanaloa has other meanings that illustrate the ultimate result when the three selves come together in perfect accord with one another: "secure," "firm," "immovable," "unconquerable," and "total confidence."

PART FOUR

HO'OPONOPONO

In order to achieve Kanaloa consciousness, we use our conscious mind as a loving and attentive parent, keeping our unconscious mind from deterring us from achieving the potential held in our superconscious mind. *Ho'oponopono*, a simple and extremely effective Hawaiian forgiveness practice, is used expressly for this purpose. Ho'oponopono helps us heal the divisions within our three selves and reclaim our wholeness, so that Ku, Lono, and Kane can unite forever in Kanaloa.

CHAPTER FOURTEEN
HO'OPONOPONO

In old Hawaii, one of the worst things you could do was hold a grudge and not grant forgiveness when it was asked of you. Refusing forgiveness was considered so offensive that you could even be exiled from the community for it. Kala and *I mua*—which mean "letting go" and "moving on," respectively—weren't just practical instructions for living well, they were also among the islanders' highest cultural values. Ho'oponopono, a powerfully transformative ancient practice, uses love, forgiveness, and mutual understanding to release pain, negativity, and limitation.

As you learned in the chapters in Part Three on the Three Selves, we sometimes have unconscious, negative memory patterns that obscure our goodness and our inherent divinity, and which can greatly hinder our lives. It is a further testament to the ancient Hawaiians' genius that Ho'oponopono was primarily practiced where those patterns tend to originate: in the family. The islanders used Ho'oponopono as a kind of family therapy, aiming the practice at releasing negative memory patterns at their source *before* they could become detrimental, fixed patterns lodged in the Ku.

Serge Kahili King calls his own family tradition of Ho'oponopono *Kupono*, which is roughly translated as "making the Ku right with itself." This is the ultimate goal of Ho'oponopono: letting go or erasing the memory patterns held in our unconscious mind that are harmful and do not serve us.

We have already touched on the seed meanings of the components of Ho'oponopono: *Ho'o* is causative, and can be thought of to mean "to make," and *pono* (which is doubled, for emphasis) means "rightness" or "true condition of Nature." Ho'oponopono, then, restores problems not only to pono (rightness), but to *ponopono* (to make amends, to correct). In other words, we use Ho'oponopono to make right, more right—and as we become right with ourselves, we become right with God.

Traditionally, Ho'oponopono was a somewhat structured and formal process. A mediator (often a Kahuna or an elder) would lead the family or group through the process. First came a prayer, which was followed by a series of prescribed steps: a formal explanation of the rules of the process, the naming of the problem to be addressed, verbal confessions and acknowledgements of any wrong doing, making amends, agreement by all parties to forgive, a closing prayer, and, finally, a celebratory meal. Ho'oponopono could go on for hours or even days until a specific problem was completely resolved, released, and forgiven; once the practice was completed, it was understood that the issue that had been resolved was never to be discussed again.

Over time, Ho'oponopono transformed into a few variations, and today it is a practice that one most often does by oneself. I believe that Ho'oponopono evolved this way because the practice's overall intention—using love and attention to release negative memory patterns—is so universal in terms of practical healing that it was easily adaptable into many other forms. The esteemed Kahuna Lapa'au (healer) Morrnah Nalamaku Simeona (1913-1992) was the strongest influence in changing Ho'oponopono into a more simplified healing practice, and the version that she taught at the World Huna Convention in 1980 is the one that is most widely practiced today. Dr. Ihaleakala Hew Len, Simeona's celebrated student, synthesized the practice even further by introducing four phrases: "I love you," "I'm sorry," "Please forgive me," and "Thank you."

Before we look at these four phrases in detail, let's review some Huna concepts as they relate to Ho'oponopono, and examine how the practice of Ho'oponopono works as well as why and when we should do it. Please understand that spiritual practice is never formulaic or mechanical. Although I describe this process in quite a linear way, it is only to appease your Lono, which might crave a more rudimentary or linear understanding.

The first principle of Huna tells us that the world is what we think it is: We create our world based on what we think, both consciously and unconsciously. If what we think consciously (Lono) is detrimental or limiting, we can consciously decide to change it. But what we think unconsciously (Ku) that is detrimental or limiting can only be changed with guidance from the conscious mind (Lono). If we can successfully change the detrimental or limiting material in the unconscious mind (Ku) so that it aligns with our higher self, or inspired potential, then the superconscious mind (Kane) engages and springs forth into the action of creating that inspired potential.

Ho'oponopono mirrors this process, and takes it a step further by using love as its primary tool. When we do Ho'oponopono, our conscious mind directs loving intentions, just like a parent would, towards unhealthy memory patterns that are held in the unconscious mind. To do this, the conscious mind uses four phrases: "I love you," "I'm sorry," "Please forgive me," and "Thank you." As Ku receives this loving attention through Lono's use of the four phrases, Ku begins to learn new beneficial patterns that erase the negative patterns, and starts to restore itself to what it always was supposed to be: divinity itself. And as Ku realizes (and memorizes) its divine nature (because Lono has guided and parented Ku to this realization), Kane is activated, raining down its creative energies on us in the form of gifts, healing, magic, and grace—or what the Hawaiians might call *mana loa.*

As I've said throughout this book, if we could see ourselves as we truly are, we would come to the realization that we are actually Godlike beings who already live in heaven. Ho'oponopono, then, is a practice in which we extend love to ourselves in order to rouse and awaken our higher self or Kane (which is in direct relation with God) to create the circumstances needed to bring about this divine realization. The Ho'oponopono practice works as well as it does because its purpose is to get our mind and body, or our Lono and our Ku, to become a unified container that is in sympathetic resonance or harmony with our God-self (Kane). That is how, when doing Ho'oponopono, we and God become one, and it is our own capacity to love that gets us there.

Because energy flows where attention goes, I will suggest some localities for Ku, Lono, and Kane so that you can think of your three selves in specific places in order to focus your attention on them when you practice Ho'oponopono. Please do not take these places too literally, as they are simply a way to help you to visualize the process. You might think of Lono living in your head, from where it sends love (through the four phrases) to Ku, which you can visualize as being in your belly and your heart. When Ku receives the loving intentions from Lono, Ku begins to move into sympathetic vibration with Kane, and enters into a kind of "communication" with it. You can imagine your Kane existing somewhere above your head, or in the sky. From above you, Kane "petitions" God, or Akua Nui, on your behalf (though we need not know how Kane does this), and the divine energies that can heal and release the problem in Ku (belly and heart) are sent down to you. The diagram that follows helps illustrate the process.

Ho'oponopono follows what I call the "down-to-go-up paradigm" of Shamanism: We find our way "up" to God by going "down" into ourselves, and this is how we invite God *to come to us*. In other words, by filling ourselves with love, we are transformed into beings who are able to receive the love of the divine, or Akua Nui. Heaven is right here because we create it with our minds, and Heaven then obliges us by making it so.

As the Hawaiians say, *E iho ana 'o luna, E pi'i ana 'o lalo*: "That which is above shall come down, that which is below shall rise up."

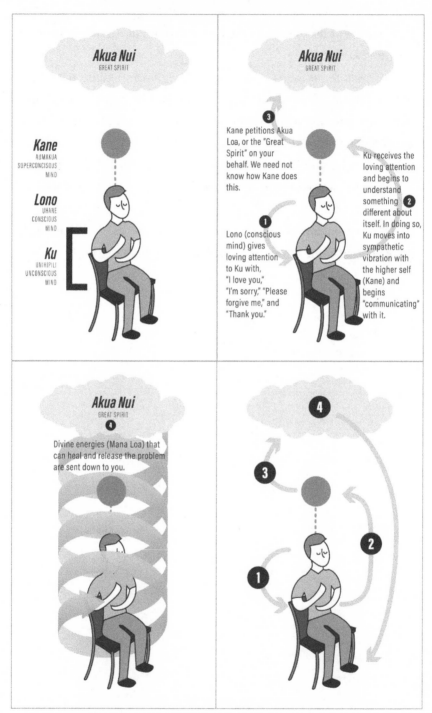

THE FOUR STEPS OF HO'OPONOPONO

As Ho'oponopono has emerged into our contemporary Western spiritual culture, the four phrases used in the practice have gone through different shifts and changes. I've heard them taught in different sequences, and a variety of different interpretive meanings have been attributed to them. Some people say you should to speak the four phrases as an affirmation, while others think of them as a repetitive mantra. Though it makes absolutely no sense to me, I've also heard some Ho'oponopono teachers say that even if you are entirely devoid of intention or emotion, all you have to do is say the phrases and you will be doing Ho'oponopono. There are even some purists who don't believe that the phrases have anything whatsoever to do with the practice, so they don't use them at all. And it seems that the Hawaiians themselves have never quite agreed upon what exactly Ho'oponopono is or isn't, in the first place.

In her book *Nana I Ke Kumu*, Hawaiian scholar and educator Mary Kawena Pukui writes that many post-Christian Hawaiians considered Ho'oponopono "a stupid heathen thing," and that if they did practice it, they often did so in secret. In her research, Pukui also found that there were many different family traditions of Ho'oponopono, as well as wildly distorted and mutated versions of the practice which had sprung up among both the islanders and many Western practitioners. Ho'oponopono has been mistakenly characterized as everything from fortunetelling to sorcery, ritualistic fasting, house blessing, and even forms of exorcism. So, like most things Hawaiian, there is no singularly "correct" Ho'oponopono.

I can only teach you the version that I know, which is also the one that has been most effective with my clients and students—effectiveness being the measure of truth, after all. The version that I teach does utilize "I love you," "I'm sorry," "Please forgive me," and "Thank you." Having facilitated Ho'oponopono for so many people, I have found that my own interpretive meanings for the four phrases have developed of their own accord, and I will share these with you, but I also encourage you to allow your own gnosis to feel into these phrases, and see if you relate to them differently.

In Ho'oponopono, we speak the four phrases to any "problem" in Ku. Think of it as using the phrases to communicate with your little one—your Ku/child, who learned and memorized something mistaken about themselves that has subsequently obscured their wholeness and their inherent divine nature. With sincerity and persistence, we use the four Ho'oponopono phrases to guide that child to a different understanding of themselves. If speaking to your child-self seems too "out there" for you (although I really encourage you to try it), you can simply make contact in whatever way you can with the hurt parts of yourself—your illness, your low-self esteem, your addictive behavior, your fear about life, your self-loathing, your bad habit—and use the phrases to extend loving attention to them.

As simple as it might sound, Ho'oponopono is so transformative because by practicing it, we give ourselves what we needed most in the first place—the thing that, had we received it, would have avoided creating the problem. What we needed most was love.

"I love you."

We begin Ho'oponopono with "I love you," because whatever problem we are addressing came about because love was withheld in some way. Negative memory patterns in Ku originate when attention, assurance, kindness, acceptance, or nurturing were not forthcoming, for whatever reason. "I love you" is how we start to fill that void inside us. It's an active way of saying, "Despite the love that you didn't receive, however you have been treated, or whatever you think yourself to be, I am here now, and *I love you.*"

There are so many different meanings of "love": We can "love" ice-cream, or we can "love" another's caustic sense of humor. But the "I love you" in Ho'oponopono is pure Aloha; it's a totally unconditional, effusively loving, fiercely supportive, and gently nurturing "I love you." The statement "I love you" becomes the new reality that you create for Ku, for the child. The child is held (and learns to hold itself) in the highest esteem and loving acceptance imaginable, and this guides them to release whatever is not in alignment with those qualities. In the face of such love, the "mistaken identity" of the problem begins to fade away, and a different way of being starts to take hold—a way of being that no longer includes the problem.

In Ho'oponopono, we say "I love you" because love is what we most need in order to not turn on ourselves. Love is the baseline; it is the new reality for Ku/the child. The love that we extend to ourselves mirrors the divine love that practicing Ho'oponopono will attract to us.

"I'm sorry."

In his book *Ho'oponopono: Your Path to True Forgiveness*, Huna teacher Dr. Matt James postulates that the ancient Hawaiians wouldn't think of saying "I'm sorry." In fact, he notes, there isn't even a way to express this sentiment precisely in their language. Operating under the cosmological standpoint that everything is connected and cooperative, the islanders might have considered the phrase "I'm sorry" to be too one-sided, because it doesn't ask for anything in return. "I'm sorry," James writes, "ends energetically about twelve inches from your mouth." So, instead of saying, "I'm sorry," the Hawaiians sought a shared experience of cooperation and common ground by asking for forgiveness.

So, if "I'm sorry" isn't quite Hawaiian, then why is it included in modern-day Ho'oponopono? When the Hawaiians of old did Ho'oponopono as a group practice, an extremely important initial step of the process was to name formally the problem to be addressed. While this might seem rather obvious, it is only when we express and name our experience that it actually becomes real. "I'm sorry" isn't about requesting forgiveness—that comes in the next phrase, "Please forgive me"—it is the compassionate acknowledgment of a problem. "I'm sorry" is a way of saying, "I see you. I see your suffering. I see your pain. I see this problem as it is, and *I am so sorry* that it is affecting you this way."

To have our hardships named is to hold them with understanding and compassion, which is a vital step toward healing them. When our suffering is seen and validated by another, we start to develop compassion for ourselves, and our self-compassion awakens our self-love. Remember that Ku takes everything personally. So when the child hears that the parent is "sorry" for the child's pain, the child learns that their suffering is real, that it matters very much, and that they are not suffering alone. "I'm sorry" helps the child learn and understand that whatever has happened to them (negative memories) that has led to their suffering is unfortunate and unfair, and that they deserved much better, but that it was never actually about them, and that it need not have anything to do with their identity.

It is through the acknowledgment of the problem that the child starts to let it go, because implied in the naming of a problem is the freedom to change it. Carl Rogers, one of the pioneers of humanistic psychology, writes in his book *On Becoming a Person: A Therapist's View of Psychotherapy,* "The curious paradox is that when I accept myself just as I am, then I can change."

In Ho'oponopono, we say "I'm sorry," in order to get real with ourselves. "I'm sorry" helps us sit squarely in our pain, because by naming it we begin the process of losing our identification with it.

"Please forgive me."

Forgiveness is the ultimate goal of Ho'oponopono. But this isn't about having your apology accepted. Forgiveness, in Ho'oponopono, is the total release and complete removal of any negative memory pattern that is anything other than our God-self. Dr. Hew Len calls this "getting back to zero," which, from his perspective, is our true nature: "Zero" is an unblemished and unstained canvas of divinity itself. We do Hoʻoponopono to erase any false imprints that obscure our divinity, so that the only thing that remains *is* divinity.

Every child comes into this world in a kind of perfection—innocent, whole, soul-intact; an individual expression of God—and then begins the process of forgetting it. This is the human condition. No matter how loving or progressive the parenting may have been, the child will inevitably react to the pain of the world by saying no to at least some aspect of themselves, and by assuming that they are in some way less than who they really are.

Though we may have not been aware of it at the time, we have all damaged ourselves in these ways, or allowed others to damage us, and once these detrimental memory patterns are in place, we start to habitually "agree" with them; we even fortify and strengthen those memories with our thoughts, actions, and beliefs. We may also ignore our negative memory patterns completely, or even be wholly unaware of them, which will cause us to suffer, sometimes for years on end. "Please forgive me" is how we take one hundred percent responsibility for any way in which we failed (intentionally or unintentionally) to do right by ourselves.

Asking the child for forgiveness is a way of saying, "While others may have wronged you, or you have wronged yourself, I allowed it or I was unaware of it, and I ask you to *please forgive me for this.*" The child learns a piece of vital information from "Please forgive me": namely, that they themselves were never the mistake. The mistake was the way in which others failed them, or the fact that the child simply had no other guidance to help them to avoid failing themselves.

"Please forgive me," is also how we start to make a new commitment to the child. In asking Ku for forgiveness, Lono is telling it, "I have not parented you well enough, please forgive me for that, and I promise to do much better in the future." In other words, from now on Lono will take care of Ku differently, with a commitment to guide it over and over again to new and more beneficial possibilities. Implied in "Please forgive me," is Lono's promise to be a much more loving and attentive guide to Ku.

But, as I am sure you have experienced in your own life, forgiving and forgetting are two entirely different things. I don't want to imply that the removal of negative memory patterns is only effective if we also somehow forget what happened to us. It doesn't work like that. Rather, forgiveness means that we are releasing the "hold" that the negative memory pattern has over us, and that we are refusing to perpetuate it further: *It happened to us but it isn't us.*

Atonement was a necessary part of Ho'oponopono because the ancient Hawaiians knew that forgiveness "sticks" by making amends. In other words, forgiveness is contingent on an agreement that if forgiveness is granted, there is a promise not only to show up differently in the future, but also to make up for the suffering that has been caused.

In traditional Hawaiian culture, *ho'ohiki*, to "make a promise," was an extremely serious business. The Hawaiians considered a promise to be an irrevocable and binding pledge that was not to be taken unless it could be kept—for a spoken word, according to author Mary Pukui was "an actual entity, an operative agent that can bring about events." If a promise was broken, Pukui writes that it was called *hua 'ōlelo* (a "broken promise" or "malicious statement") which was thought to be punished with misfortune, illness, or even death. This is one of the most important concepts in understanding Ho'oponopono: True forgiveness only happens when we make the choice never to aid in our own suffering again, and we make a vow to pay off the debt of our transgressions by gifting the child with kindness, love, and attention in the future.

I often tell my clients, "Your child has been through enough, don't you dare put them through more." In fact, what the child deserves from you is nothing short of the moon and the stars. In his classes, Dr. Hew Len often speaks of "incessant Ho'oponopono," which means that if you are truly making amends to the child, then you must practice a constant Ho'oponopono with them with your words, actions, and deeds. In asking for forgiveness, Lono makes a commitment to give perpetual loving attention to Ku—so much attention, in fact, that when Dr. Hew Len was asked in one of his classes what he considered to be "enough" Ho'oponopono, he shrugged and said, "It's tedious."

In Ho'oponopono, we say, "Please forgive me" in order to take responsibility for any wrongdoing (ours and others), to make a new commitment to the child, and to promise to make amends in the future.

"Thank you."

We say thank you to the child to express our gratitude to it. The child learned to adapt, to make sense of the world, and to get its needs met however it could. As we have discussed, the child may have learned to close down on their body, to create a false sense of self, even to develop addictive behaviors or any number of other negative patterns. But these adaptations were necessary and effective at the time, and they were often the best ways in which the child knew to cope. So, we offer "Thank you" to the child to let them know that, even in their mistakes, they were always doing their best. No matter how far they may have veered from their true (and divine) self, we want the child to know that they did an amazing job.

By framing the child's negative adaptations with "Thank you," we are suggesting that just as the child once chose a non-beneficial pattern, they can now choose a more positive one. In this way, we thank Ku for agreeing to adopt the new reality that Lono is presenting to it. Extending gratitude to the child is as a way of saying, "While I haven't been here in the way that you needed me to be, I am now. *Thank you* for waiting for me, *thank you* for letting me take care of you now, and *thank you* for following my guidance in letting this problem go."

Lastly, "Thank you" is the last of the four phrases, because "Thank you" has a sense of finality to it. You might also think of "Thank you" as expressing a sense of completion to the Ho'oponopono process that is something like "Amen," "So it is," or "It is done."

In Ho'oponopono, we say "thank you" to offer gratitude for past mistakes and for the allowance of new blessings, and to affirm that the work is complete.

Ho'oponopono and the Unitive Consciousness of the Shaman's Mind

The shaman's mind sees everything as interconnected and interdependent: Everything is a reflection of everything else, what exists in you also exists in the other, and what exists in the other also exists in you. In other words, according to the unitive consciousness of the shaman, my problems are inside you, and your problems are inside me. To take this a step further, if the world is a reflection of my thoughts (or your thoughts), then I hold the *cause* of your problem, and you hold the cause of mine. Likewise, whatever I heal inside of myself, I also heal in you and vice versa.

When we use Ho'oponopono to erase a negative memory pattern within ourselves, we remove a blemish on the collective soul of us *all*. The more that each of us returns to what Dr. Hew Len calls "a state of zero," the more everyone else does too. We have to accept one hundred percent responsibility for ourselves, because whatever individual actions we take, they have direct ramifications on the collective. Given the sheer scale and magnitude of the holistic view of reality that the shaman's mind holds, Ho'oponopono is not just something that you do for yourself—it is an altruistic act that benefits all beings.

If you recall, the shaman is defined by their ultimate purpose—the preservation and stewardship of the Earth and all of its inhabitants.

Ho'oponopono is a distinctly shamanic practice because it directly aligns with that purpose. If there is a problem inside you that is something other than your God-self, you do Ho'oponopono with yourself to heal it. And, listen up now: If there is a problem outside of you that is something other than its god-self, then we can assume that it is a reflection of something inside of you, and you *also* do Ho'oponopono with yourself.

Ho'oponopono is the final destination of the shaman's mind, because the very nature of what it can do requires us to take ownership of the individual power that we each have to make a substantive, transformative impact on the world. Each of us has the power and capability to bring all beings back to their divinity. In other words, *the divine realization of all sentient beings starts and ends with you.*

The Hawaiians tell us to "Love yourself as you love would love God," and, according to Ho'oponopono, in doing so *you are creating more God for everyone else.* If you have the power to create God, then that means that you *are* God. And the parts of you can't quite believe this about yourself simply need to hear, "I love you," "I'm sorry," "Please forgive me," and "Thank you" often enough until they finally get it, and come home to the truth.

Ho'oponopono — Individual Practice

As with all the practices in this book, there is no "right way" to practice Ho'oponopono. I am sharing with you what has worked well for me, but you may choose to adapt it however you are internally guided. I tend to think of Ho'oponopono as a continuation of the inner-child work that we did in Chapter Twelve (Lono), but it is enough to know that whatever you seek to heal exists as a pattern in your body-mind, and that all you have to do is to focus your attention on the problem (or the child that learned to hold the problem), and allow the process to unfold as it will.

As you are prompted through this practice, you do not necessarily need to speak the four phrases out loud; it is sufficient to just communicate Hoʻoponopono through your thoughts.

You can do this practice seated upright or lying down. The most important thing is to be very comfortable, so if you are sitting up, allow yourself to lean back and sink into your chair. Hoʻoponopono is extremely self-nurturing, so it is important that you be as comfortable and gentle with yourself as possible.

I encourage you to record the following text while speaking slowly, and make sure you give yourself a little "dead space," or pause, at the end of each paragraph so that you have enough time for your internal experience. Or, you can read it over a few times to get the overall gist of it, and then communicate the four phrases in your own way.

Begin by closing your eyes, and allowing your consciousness and attention to go inward. Feel that you are fully inside your body. If the body is the temple, then you are sitting or lying down in the temple. Place one hand on your energetic heart at the very center of your chest, and the other hand on your lower belly.

Breathe.

Become gently aware of your hands touching your body. Tune into them. You might feel heat, tingling, or a kind of energy emanating from your hands, or you might simply be aware of the gentle pressure of your hands on your body. Allow the touch of your hands on your body to help you make deep inward contact with yourself.

Breathe.

Now imagine that the energy, heat or touch of your hands is coming from the most loving, kind, and nurturing mother. This mother is fiercely protective; she is your biggest advocate, and she loves you unconditionally. Allow yourself to receive her warmth and tenderness. Imagine that it is her love that emanates from your hands on your body.

This mother embodies the conscious mind (Lono), which is making the choice right now to care for the child. Let your mind be filled with the warmest and most loving and nurturing energy; a perfect mother's love is touching and holding you now. Allow yourself to receive this love.

Breathe.

The subconscious mind (Ku) is the child, or the aspect of you that is holding the problem or struggle that you wish to address. As you touch your body now, you are relating directly to Ku. Ku is carrying the child's burden. If you have depression, it is a memory in the child that has caused it. If you have issues with self-esteem, the child holds this too. If you feel undeserving, unworthy, or unlovable, the child has memory patterns that make it feel undeserving, unworthy, or unlovable. If you have a difficult time expressing yourself or feeling your feelings, if you feel ungrounded, or if you feel that that you don't quite belong in this world, it is because Ku learned and memorized these things.

At one time, probably very long ago, you adapted to your environment by holding something in your body that shouldn't be there, or by constricting against yourself, or by sending parts of yourself away. The child/Ku holds these mistakes, and we are going to begin the process of making all of this right again.

Breathe.

Let the child know that you are acknowledging their presence totally. In the past, you may have forgotten them some of the time, or even quite often. Perhaps you have even ignored, hurt, or scared the child, or maybe you have not even known that they were there. But you are here now, you are in charge, and you are taking full responsibility for their care. Whatever problem you are addressing, it's the result of love being withheld, and you are here now to give your love so that the child can start to let that problem go. Focus your full attention on the problem, and on the child who learned to hold it.

Breathe.

Now, speak directly to the child and the problem that they hold, and tell them, "I love you." With as much sincerity and earnestness as you can muster, tell them again, "I love you. I. Love. You." Say to them, "That was then, and this is now, and I am here now, and I love you." Tell them one more time, "I love you."

Breathe.

And let the energy of your hands, as if your hands were touching this child's body, convey to them, "I love you." Let them feel "I love you" through your hands.

Breathe.

And now, tell the child part of you, "I'm sorry. I am so sorry." Tell them, "I see this problem clearly, I see your suffering, and I'm sorry that you were treated in this way. I'm sorry that you have been made to feel the way that you have, and I'm so sorry that you ever thought that this memory was something about you. You learned a mistake about yourself. None of this was fair to you, and I'm so sorry about it."

Breathe.

Let the energy of your hands, as if your hands were touching this child's little body, convey to them, "I'm sorry". Let them feel "I'm sorry" through your hands. Tell them one more time, "I love you, and say to them again, "I'm sorry."

Breathe.

And now, ask this child, "Please forgive me." Say to this part of you, "Please forgive me for not being there for you, or for not knowing how to protect you. In any way in which I have not done right by you, please forgive me." And, in your own words, tell this part of you exactly how you will make amends to it in the future if it grants you forgiveness. Do that now.

Breathe.

Let the energy of your hands, as if your hands were touching this child's little body, convey to them, "Please forgive me." Let them feel "Please forgive me" through your hands. Tell them one more time, "I love you." Say to them, "I'm sorry," and ask them again, "Please for-give me."

Breathe.

And now, tell the child, "Thank you." Say to this part of you, "Thank you for always doing your best, and thank you for trying so hard. Thank you for being open to receive what I am giving you now. Thank you for receiving my love. Thank you for letting go of this problem now. Thank you."

Breathe.

Let the energy of your hands convey your gratitude, as if your hands were touching this child's little body. Let them feel "Thank you" through your hands. Tell them again, "I love you." Say to them, "I'm sorry." Ask them again, "Please forgive me," and say to them, "Thank you."

Breathe.

With your hands still touching your own heart and belly, lovingly speak the four phrases a few more times to your child-self, to that ten-der place within you that holds the problem. As you do this, start to become gently aware of the space around your physical body, particu-larly at your head and your shoulders. Although you have been focus-ing inwardly, sense the space around you.

As you hold this child with love, you'll begin to notice that there is a divine presence holding you—an energy, a grace, or a healing light is starting to surround you.

Feel into these healing energies around you. Open yourself to them and let your child feel them too. Something outside of you is offering you the same loving energy that you have been offering your child. Feel this love as a celestial light that is swirling around you. Take it in. Breathe it in and receive its radiant luminescence, and hear it convey to you that it loves you. Feel it tell you that it is so sorry. Know that it is asking for your forgiveness, and sense that it is offering its thanks to you.

The love that you have extended to the child inside of you is now being extended to you by your higher self. As below, so above.

Breathe.

There is only one energy now—one love—feel it within and without. That which is above shall come down, that which is below shall rise up.

Kane's grace, the mana loa, is flowing down to you. Open up to it, and allow it to remove and release the problem, dissolving it into nothingness.

Abide in Kanaloa consciousness as you feel Ku, Lono, and Kane unite together in harmony, tenderness, and bliss. Take in the powerful healing light of the mana loa, and come home. Keep repeating the four phrases as you will.

Breathe.

Stay in this graceful state as long as you like, and when you feel complete, say "Thank you," one last time, open your eyes, and come back into your space.

You may wish to record your experience of this practice in a journal.

Ho'oponopono is a map that teaches us how to live a spiritual life. While it is certainly beneficial to present it as an individual spiritual practice, the real power and the ultimate benefit of what Ho'oponopono can accomplish for you comes not by practicing it, but by living it.

There are no limits. The soul's journey is an endless one, and the collective healing that all of humanity needs is boundless and inconceivable. There is no end to the work, because even when we make individual progress with ourselves, it is only to reveal one more layer of the mistaken identity of our godlessness, followed by even more layers. The Hawaiians call this *Mahiki*, which means "to peel off" or "to scrape the bark of a tree to judge the wood beneath," and it refers to how we use Ho'oponopono to peel back that which obscures the truth only to reveal another layer of the problem. The real truth is the natural perfection of every single one of us, but the depth of our forgetfulness of this truth knows no bounds.

Given the magnitude of the challenge of what each of us is up against in pursuit of wholeness, my wish for you is to aspire for a lifetime of Ho'oponopono. This means that "I love you," "I'm sorry," "Please forgive me," and "Thank you," inform and guide every step you take, every action you make, and every person that you chose to invite into your life. This is a constant and forever promise that you make to yourself to always do whatever you possibly can to never lock yourself out of your own heart, put yourself in dangerous situations or ignore the fact that you are real, that you are precious, and that you matter so very much.

Find your own Hawaii. Give yourself your own paradise. And when you do, you will discover that you don't even need it, for you are already beyond.

AFTERWORD

I had just arrived in Maui, and I had one more chapter of this book left to write. Having been to Hawaii many times, Domenic and I have the process of traveling there down to a science. As soon as we're off the plane, he gets the bags from the baggage claim, and I beat the crowd by jumping on the rental car shuttle, so I'm the first one in line from our plane to get our car. I pick him up on the short strip in front of the airport, and off we go. We need no maps or GPS; we know exactly where we are. Maui is like a comfy sweater—it's so familiar to us now, and it feels like home.

On that particular trip, it was already about 5:00 p.m. when we landed in Maui. After almost fourteen hours of travel, and despite feeling a bit dirty and dusty, we decided to drive to our condo, drop off our stuff, throw on our flip-flops and shorts, and head to one of our favorite beaches to watch the sunset.

We arrived at Kewakapu Beach around forty-five minutes later, a beach we had visited probably close to a hundred occasions. Despite my familiarity with this place, as soon as I descended the steps from the parking lot onto the beach, felt my toes in the sand, and sat down to get my bearings, I took just one look around, and I was awestruck.

The sun was close to the horizon, and its position cast a shadowy backlit effect on the neighboring island of Lanai that made it glow in the distance. The vast ocean expanse held various shades of purple, blue, turquoise, and black, and specks of light on the water appeared and disappeared in flickering patterns of kaleidoscopic radiance.

To my right, all the way down the coastline, the verdant, emerald green jungles of the enormous West Maui Mountains jutted outward dramatically into the sea. The mountains were covered with wisps of mists and thick white, gray, and black clouds that caught the sun in such a way that it made the mountains seem ephemeral, as if these huge masses of earth were somehow unattached to the ground and floating, hovering over the ocean.

The vast expanse of sky was an endless horizon of green, gray, and blue that had an other-worldly luminosity, and the faint outline of a daytime moon hung so low in the sky that I could practically touch it. The palm trees "clicked" with welcoming messages of Aloha, the waves lapped and sprayed gently, and the winds whispered all around my face and body.

Tears began to well up in my eyes. I had been there so many times, and yet it was brand new again. Maybe I was experiencing Hawaii differently now after being enmeshed in writing this book for so many months. Or it could be that the endless hours of connecting with the islands in my mind had shifted something inside me that caused me to see them with a different set of eyes. In the moments that followed, I knew that I was not on a beautiful island in the middle of the South Pacific, but I was in the cloud-capped crystal palace that shamans call "the upper world," and the Hawaiians refer to as Lanikeha, which means "the highest heaven."

I took everything in with all my senses, and as my consciousness altered slightly into a shaman's mind, I began to contemplate my life:

"How did I get to this place? How did Hawaii become my physical destination, and the destination of my consciousness? Why am I so fortunate to experience this? Is there any end to the delight that this place brings me?"

At that moment, I felt a presence next to me. I turned, and there, sitting next to me, was me at about five years old. I watched him looking up at the sky, and he too was taking in all that I was experiencing. He turned to me and said, "None of this is for you. It's for me. You did this for me. You took care of me, and that's why we're here."

We sat next to each other for some time. I cried. He rolled his eyes at me, slightly judgmental of my mushy sentimentality. And that was that.

Aloha.

BIBLIOGRAPHY

Adyashanti. *Falling into Grace.* Boulder, CO: Sounds True, 2013

Allen, Jeffrey. *Duality.* Kuala Lumpur, Malaysia: Mindvalley Academy, 2015

Becker, Catherine & Doya Nardin. *Mana Cards, The Power of Hawaiian Wisdom.* Hilo, HI: Radiance Network, 1998

Beckwith, Martha. *The Kumulipo: A Hawaiian Creation Chant.* Honolulu, HI: University of Hawaii Press, 1951

Beckwith, Martha. *Hawaiian Mythology.* Honolulu, HI: University of Hawaii Press,1970 and 2009

Berney, Charlotte. *Fundamentals of Hawaiian Mysticism.* New York, NY: Crossing Press, 2000

Bodin, Luc, Nathalie Bodin Lamboy & Jean Graciet. *The Book of Ho'oponopono.* Rochester, VT: Destiny Books, 2012

Brach, Tara. *Radical Acceptance, Embracing your Life with the Heart of the Buddha.* New York, NY: Bantam Dell, 2003

Cunningham, Scott. *Hawaiian Magic and Spirituality.* Woodbury, MN: Llewellyn Publications, 2002

Ingerman, Sandra. *Walking in Light.* Boulder, CO: Sounds True, 2014

James, Dr. Matt. *The Foundation of Huna.* Kailua-Kona, HI: Advanced Neuro Dynamics, 2014

James, Dr. Matt. *Ho'oponopono: Your Path to True Forgiveness.* Carlsbad, CA: Crescendo Publishing, 2017

Jung, Carl. *Psychology and Alchemy (Collected Works of C.G. Jung Vol. 12).* Princeton, NJ: Princeton University Press, 1980

Ka 'ano 'i, Patrick. *Kamalamalama: The Light of Knowledge.* Las Vegas, NV: Ka 'ano 'I Publishing, 2008

Kanahele, Dr. Pualani Kanaka'ole. *Ha'ena: Intense Breath of the Sun.* Honolulu, Hi: Ted Talks x Honolulu, 2012

King, Serge Kahili. *Changing Reality.* Wheaton, IL: Quest Books, 2013

King, Serge Kahili. *Endless Energy.* Volcano, HI: Hunaworks, 2009

King, Serge Kahili. *Huna: Ancient Hawaiian Secrets for Modern Living.* New York, NY: Atria Books, 2008

King, Serge Kahili. *Kahuna Healing.* Wheaton, IL: Quest Books, 1983

King, Serge Kahili. *Instant Healing.* New York, NY: St. Martin's Press, 2008

King, Serge Kahili. *Mastering Your Hidden Self.* Wheaton, IL: Quest Books, 1990

King, Serge Kahili. *Urban Shaman.* New York, NY: Atria Books, 1990

Kupihea, Moke. *Kahuna of Light.* Rochester, VT: Inner Traditions, 2001

Levy, Paul. *Dispelling Watiko: Breaking the Curse of Evil.* Berkeley, CA: North Atlantic Books, 2013

Long, Max Freedom. *The Huna Code in Religions.* Marina del Ray, CA: DeVross & Co., 1965

Long, Max Freedom. *The Secret Science Behind Miracles.* Marina del Ray, CA: DeVross & Co., 1948 and 2009

Mackinnon, Christa. *Shamanism.* Carlsbad, CA: Hay House, 2016

Morrel, Rima. *The Hawaiian Oracle.* Novato, CA: New World Library, 2006

Morrel, Rima. *The Sacred Power of Huna.* Rochester, VT: Inner Traditions, 2005

Myss, Caroline. *Anatomy of the Spirit.* New York, NY: Harmony Publishing, 1996

Myss, Caroline. *Sacred Contracts: Awaking your Divine Potential.* Boulder, CO: Sounds True, 2001

Perkins, John. *Shapeshifting: Shamanic Techniques for Global and Personal Transformation.* Rochester, VT: Destiny Books, 1997.

Pukui, Mary & Samuel H. Elbert. *Hawaiian Dictionary.* Honolulu, HI: University of Hawaii Press, 1986

Pukui, Mary. *Nana I Ke Kumu (Look to the Source). Volumes 1 and 2.* Honolulu, HI: Queen Lili 'uokalani Children's Center, 1972 and 1979

Roberts, Llyn. *Shamanic Reiki.* New Alresford, UK: Moon Books, 2007

Roberts, Llyn. *Shapeshifting into Higher Consciousness.* New Alresford, UK: Moon Books, 2011

Rogers, Carl. *On Becoming a Person: A Therapist's View of Psychotherapy.* Wilmington, MA: Mariner Books, 1995

Segal, Eran. *The Perfect Diet for Humans.* Ruppin, Israel: Ted Talks x Ruppin, June 23, 2016

Shook, Victoria. *Ho'oponopono.* Honolulu, HI: University of Hawaii Press, 1986

Sonea, Sorin. *The Global Organism.* New York, NY: New York Academy of Sciences, Volume 28 - Issue 4, 1988

Stein, Diane. *Essential Reiki.* Berkeley, CA: Crossing Press, 1995

Vitale, Joe & Ihaleakala Hew Len. *Zero Limits.* Hoboken, NJ: Wiley & Sons, 2008

Watts, Alan. *Out of your Mind.* Boulder, CO: Sounds True, 2004

Wesselman, Hank. *The Bowl of Light.* Boulder, CO: Sounds True, 2011

Wesselman, Hank & Jill Kuykendall. *Spirit Medicine.* Carlsbad, CA: Hay House, 2004

ABOUT THE AUTHOR

Jonathan Hammond is a teacher, energy healer, shamanic practitioner, and spiritual counselor. Before beginning his work in holistic health and spirituality, he had a career as an award-winning actor, appearing on Broadway and on television.

A graduate of Harvard University and the University of Michigan, Jonathan is a certified Master Teacher in Shamanic Reiki, Usui, and Karuna Reiki, and the advanced graduate studies advisor for Shamanic Reiki Worldwide. He teaches classes in Shamanism, energy healing, spirituality, and Huna at the Omega Institute for Holistic Studies and around the world.

Jonathan has training and certifications in Cherokee Bodywork, Huna, and Ho'oponopono, and is an ordained Alakai (leader or guide) through Aloha International. He has completed the core curriculum studies at the Foundation for Shamanic Studies, and has been initiated through the Minoan Fellowship in Wicca.

In addition to his background in energy medicine, Jonathan completed four years of training at One Spirit Learning Alliance (OSLA) in New York City, and was ordained as an interfaith minister in 2008. He is currently a faculty member at OSLA, where he teaches Shamanism and interspiritual counseling, and he is the founding leader of OSLA's monthly shamanic circle. Jonathan has also studied Shamanism, energy healing, and meditation privately, with prominent teachers in North and South America, and has worked alongside shamans in Mexico, Brazil, Bali, Costa Rica, Nicaragua, and Hawaii.

Jonathan now spends his life deeply committed to empowering and healing people by bringing indigenous Earth wisdom to the modern world, and leads international spiritual retreats through his company, The Living Project. *The Shaman's Mind: Huna Wisdom to Change your Life* is his first book. He lives in New York City with his husband Domenic and his rambunctious pug, Lord Bartholomew Archer.

ACKNOWLEDGMENTS

There are so many people that made this book possible, and there is no way that I can possibly express my gratitude to all of them. Nevertheless, I'll do my best here.

I want to thank my main teachers, Serge Kahili King and Llyn Roberts, my beloved mentor and savior Brian McCormack, and my family.

In addition, I want to thank Stacey Gibbons and Emily Wallace for being amazing colleagues and friends, as well as James Donegan, Rianne Vestuto, Bobby Steggert, Sarah Bowen, David Ito, Nikki Rubin, and Huna-extraordinaire Peter Dalton for reading this book in its early stages and offering their wonderful insights. And, to my astonishing first editor, John Breeze: Your guidance transformed this project into something so much better than what I had imagined, and I offer you my humble thanks.

I am forever indebted to the entire team at Monkfish Book Publishing Company. I offer my sincerest thanks to publisher Paul Cohen, to my genius editor Susan Piperato, and to my designer Colin Rolfe.

Thank you to James Donegan for creating the "Steps to Ho'oponopono " illustrations in Chapter Fourteen.

Thank you to Jeffrey Allen for allowing me to adapt his "Permission Rose" meditation for this book.

To my clients and students, past and present: You are all extraordinary and I continue to learn from you every day. To everyone who has touched my life and shaped me in any way, please know that my heart holds every one of you.

To all the authors and teachers who were included in the bibliography of this book, you have been with me for years despite your not knowing it.

Thank you to Hawaii and its people. I promise to do my part to take care of you.

And, finally, to my beloved Domenic, who made my entire life Hawaii so that I could give a little bit of Hawaii to the world. This book would never have happened without you. You are my best friend, the greatest gift I could ever hope to receive, and the light of my life.

aka	A vast etheric field of potential
akaku	Vision, trance, hallucination
akua	The gods or goddesses, or the god or goddess (also "spirit," in the sense of essence)
Aloha	The fifth principle: to love is to be happy with. Also, love, compassion, affection, mercy, sympathy, kindness, grace, charity
Ana'ana	Black magic, evil sorcery
ano'ai	Greetings, salutations for the perhaps unexpected
Ao	Light, day, visible or manifest reality
Aumakua	Guardian spirit, the ancestors (similar to Kane or the higher self)
'E'epa	Trickery, deceit that passes comprehension, mischievous spirits
Eha'eha	Pain and suffering
Ha	The breath of life, spirit
Ha'ena	Extreme heat, hot sun, intense breath
hailona	A divination involving casting stones, shells, dice

Haleakala	Maui's dormant volcano ("House of the Sun")
Hana Aloha	The love prayer
Haole	A white or Caucasian person (formerly any foreigner)
hapai	pregnant
Haumuna	A student
hoʻailona	Omens, signs
Hoʻo	To make (causative)
hoʻohiki	To make a promise
Hoʻomana	To empower; religion, church
Hoʻoponopono	The Hawaiian forgiveness process; to straighten something out or make it right
hoaka	The human energetic field, or aura
Honi	Sharing breath with another, nose to nose; used today for "kiss"
Hu	To rise or swell, to percolate, to surge or rise to the surface
hua ʻōlelo	A broken promise, an affront to a family aumakua, verbal transgression
Hula	Indigenous dance of Hawaii
Huna	The esoteric knowledge and philosophy of Hawaii, hidden secret wisdom
I mua	Moving on, forward
Ike	The first principle: The world is what you think it is. Also: to see, to know, to recognize, to perceive, to experience, to be aware
ʻIwa	A frigate bird
ka	To send out on a vine
Kahi	To press or stroke, as in massage (healing touch from the Kahili tradition)
Kahuna	An expert in some aspect of Hawaiian culture
Kahuna nui heʻe nalu	Expert surfer
Kahuna kalaiwaʻa	Expert canoe builder
Kahuna Kapua	Master shaman
Kahuna kumu hula	Hula instructor

Kahuna lapa'au	Master healer/herbalist
Kala	The second principle: There are no limits. Also: to loosen, untie, free, release, unburden, let go, undo
Kala kupua	Magic, under the control of a mysterious or supernatural power
Kane	Our higher self, superconscious mind, the god of high places/creator god
Kanehunamoku	Kane's hidden island
kaona	The hidden meanings in Hawaiian words
kapu kai	A ceremonial bath for spiritual purification (usually in the sea)
kihei	A shawl, cape
kino	The human body, a highly energized thought form
Ku	The unconscious body-mind; also, a god of war, hunting, and gathering
kuleana	Personal responsibility
kumu	The foundation, basis, teacher
Kumulipo	Hawaiian creation chant
Kupua	A magical being, equivalent to a shaman
Lanikeha	The highest heaven or the upper world
Lei	A garland, necklace of flowers
Lemuria	Another name for the lost continent, Mu, used primarily by non-Hawaiians
loa	Great, tall, excessive
lomilomi	Hawaiian massage
Lono	The conscious mind; the god of medicine and agriculture; also, news
Mahalo	Thank you
mahiki	To peel off, to scrape the bark of a tree to judge the wood beneath
ma'i	Sickness, tension
Makia	The third principle: Energy flows where attention goes. Also, to concentrate, aim, strive

Mana	The sixth principle: All power comes from within. Also, the power to create, to empower, to influence
manamana	To empower
mana loa	The highest form (divine) of Mana
Mana'o	Thought
mana'o'i'o	To have faith or confidence, to believe
manaiakalani	Maui's magical fishhook
manawa	The fourth principle: Now is the moment of power. Also, a period of time, turn, date, season, chronology
Menehune	Dwarflike people/spirits, possible descendants from the lost continent of Mu
Mu	A lost continent in the Pacific
Na	Calmed, pacified, soothed
Na'au	Guts, intestines, heart of the mind, second brain
ola	Health, a state of being healed
pala'au	To heal, as with herbs
Pachacuti	An interval of 500 years, according to the Quechua tradition
paulele	Faith, confidence, trust; literally, "stop jumping around."
pikopiko	A breathing technique from the Kahili tradition
Po	Night, darkness, the realm of the gods, invisible
Po'e aumakua	The great company of ancestors
Pono	The seventh principle: Effectiveness is the measure of truth. Also, goodness, rightness, true condition of Nature, right, beneficial, accurate, correct
ponopono	To make amends, to correct
pule	Prayer
Tapa	Cloth made from bark
Ti leaves	Leaves from a Hawaiian plant

uhane	Ghost, guiding spirit (alternative word for the conscious mind, Lono)
ulaleo	Supernatural voices
unihipili	The spirit of a dead person believed to be present in the bones or hair of the deceased and kept lovingly; also, a word sometimes for the unconscious mind
waena	A garden, center or medial
Wai	Water, liquid
Waikiki	The capital city of Oahu
Watiko	A wicked spirit, a parasite of the human psyche

9 781948 626217